When 2 + 2

When 2 + 2 = 5
Reflecting Love in a Loveless World

THE PRACTICE OF *A COURSE IN MIRACLES*

Kenneth Wapnick, Ph.D.

Foundation for A COURSE IN MIRACLES®

Foundation for A Course in Miracles®
41397 Buecking Drive
Temecula, CA 92590
www.facim.org

First printing, 2013

Printed in the United States of America

Cataloging-in-Publication Data available from the Library of Congress

CONTENTS

Preface

This book is entirely based on a full-day workshop I gave in August 2005 at our Foundation, entitled "When 2 + 2 = 5." The title is taken from Dostoesky's *Notes from Underground*, as I explain below in the Introduction. This arithmetic metaphor served as the framework for a discussion that contrasted the world's laws of differences, based on bodies, with the Holy Spirit's law of sameness of mind. This shift in focus, reflected by a shift in identity from body to mind, allows us to be healed of the belief in separation— first from each other, and ultimately from God. Gently we are led by Jesus from the 2 + 2 = 4 outer world of hate-filled differences to the 2 + 2 = 5 inner world of sameness, the home of forgiveness that reflects the universe of love and oneness, our true home of 1 + 1 = 1.

As is our custom in this series on "The Practice of *A Course in Miracles*," the lecture has been gently edited to ensure readability; at the same time we have striven to maintain the informality and spontaneity of the original workshop. Some questions and answers from that workshop have also been included, and edited in similar fashion to the lecture. Finally, we have included in the Appendix an article of the same name that appeared the following year in the *Lighthouse,* the Foundation newsletter.

Acknowledgments

I have often written in these "little books" of my deep appreciation and gratitude to Rosemarie LoSasso, the Foundation's Director of Publications, and my wife, Gloria, for their immense contribution to this series of books, indeed, all of my books. I shall not repeat myself here, except to acknowledge once again Rosemarie's wonderful ability to take the raw material of a workshop or class and mold it into a coherent and readable whole, and Gloria's original and ongoing inspiration for these "little books," unceasing reminders to do them when I dragged my feet, and her loving presence in my life for over thirty years.

1. Introduction:
Dostoevsky's Underground Man

This is the second time I have given a workshop or talk on this subject. The first was in the late 1960s. A friend of mine was teaching a graduate class in education and asked if I would speak to her class, since at that time I was directing a school program for disturbed children. I agreed and chose as the title of my talk, "2 + 2 = 5." I do not remember what I said, but am sure it was to stress that not only was it important to teach children that 2 + 2 = 4, it was also essential to teach them how to be "outside the box," where 2 + 2 = 5. I felt strongly that our educational system needed to stimulate children's creativity at as early an age as possible.

The idea of 2 + 2 = 5 did not originate with me. I came across it first in Fyodor Dostoevsky's powerful short novel, *Notes from Underground*. Dostoevsky, as you may know, was a late-nineteenth-century Russian novelist, and it is an extraordinary historical note that Tolstoy lived at the same time—two Russian literary giants! Written in 1864, Notes from Underground was Dostoevsky's first truly successful work, and one of the modern world's most influential books.

1. Introduction: Dostoevsky's Underground Man

It was the inspiration for the twentieth-century movement known as literary existentialism: fiction based on existential heroes. An existential hero is essentially someone who questions the meaning of his or her existence, a thoughtful person who realizes something in the world is not right. The underground man, unnamed in the book, is such a man.

Notes from Underground consists of the musings of a strange and disturbed person who writes a kind of diary of his thoughts about the world and society. The word *underground* in this context refers both to the idea of an antisocial, rebellious attitude, and to the underground of one's existence, what Freud would later call the unconscious. The father of psychoanalysis, in fact, had tremendous respect for Dostoevsky, who he actually thought was a greater psychologist than he. The "underground" to Freud was a reservoir of feelings and thoughts that society treats with disdain. Nietzsche also felt indebted to the great novelist.

The novel is in two parts, the first consisting of the underground man's diatribes, and the second taking the reader back 15 years to his earlier life. The key event there was his encounter with a prostitute whom he wanted to redeem. He took her into his apartment and it turned out that she had much more integrity and self-respect than he did. Though there was no sexual activity at all, he wanted to pay her but she would not take his money. That is how the novel ends. He was a demented, sick, poor excuse for a person—hardly a paragon of spiritual virtue—despite having such acute observations of society.

At this point in his life Dostoevsky was quite pessimistic. He knew the world did not work, but was not even sure it could work. His wonderful novel *The Idiot* is about an epileptic prince who goes temporarily insane; thus "the idiot." He is a sort of Christ figure despite his madness, and the book ends in tragedy—murder, insanity, and treachery. The message, if I remember correctly after so many years, was that the world was not ready for someone like Jesus: for look what it does to love and innocence. Dostoevsky felt that Jesus was the ultimate answer, but that the world could not accept his message, which is why the Church flourished by concealing the true man and his true message. I will return to this theme below.

Dostoevsky became a radical and a socialist. He was arrested and sentenced to death, but the sentence was commuted. He later turned against socialism, feeling that society held no easy answers. He did not like what was happening in Russia, but he believed there were no easy or rational answers. One of the most important themes in *Notes from Underground* is the underground man's rantings and ravings about how insane this world is, a world where $2 + 2 = 4$. Dostoevsky was attempting to say that staying with reason and rationality is a way of imprisoning us, denying us our true freedom. In that sense, again, the underground man was the first existential hero,[*] certainly in modern literature. The influence of this book, again, was extraordinary.

Note:

It was not until I looked at the book again—my first reading having been close to fifty years ago—that I realized Dostoevsky actually says 2 *times* 2 makes 4. I have always said 2 *plus* (or *and*) 2 *is* (or *equals*) 4, so I will stay with that, even though I am going to read a brief excerpt where he says 2 times 2 makes 4. The point is clear, however.

---

[*] Kierkegaard is considered to be the father of existentialism, but *Notes* is generally regarded as the first existentialist fictional novel.

2. *Notes from Underground* – Excerpts

The excerpts* that follow give an idea of how often Dostoevsky talks about two times two makes four, which for him was a symbol of the world's laws. He deplores these laws and how rigidly they keep us in check and deny our creativity and feelings. In these excerpts the underground man has been speaking about the laws of nature, the conclusions of the natural sciences and mathematics. Then he says:

> You've got to take it [the world] as it is. There's nothing else to do, because two times two is mathematics. Go argue with that.

He continues sarcastically.

> "For goodness sakes," they'll yell at you. "You can't rebel. This is two times two makes four. Nature doesn't ask your approval. She doesn't care about your desires and whether you like her laws or not. You have to take her as she is and consequently all her conclusions as well. A wall, then, is a wall," [etc., etc.] Good Lord! What do I care about the laws of nature and arithmetic? If for some reason, I

---

* NY: Thomas Y. Crowell Company, 1969; pp. 12f, 31, 33.

> do not like these laws and this two times two makes four, of course I won't ram through such a law with my head if I really do not have the strength to ram through it. But I will not submit just because I have a stone wall before me and I do not have enough strength.

In other words, our "hero" is telling the world, "Don't tell me what I can do and what I can't do. Even if there is a stone wall, I still have freedom."

> As if such a stone wall really were any solace and really did contain the slightest word of conciliation. For the one and only reason that it represents, two times two makes four. All absurdity of all absurdities.

A few pages later:

> You shout at me that, after all, no one is divesting me of my will. The only concern here is to arrange things somehow so that my will, all by itself, would of its own will, coincide with my normal advantages, with the laws of nature and with arithmetic.

Namely, that I be a good boy and do what the world says.

> Odd, gentlemen. What kind of will of one's own is that going to be when things come to tables and arithmetic? When there will be only two times two makes four around? My will or not, two times two would still be four. Some free will that is.

In other words, he is saying, "How can I have freedom if the world tells me what the laws are and defines the boundaries of my existence?"

Finally, and this is probably the most important of the excerpts:

> And who knows? Maybe the entire goal here on earth toward which mankind is striving consists of nothing more than this continuity of process of attainment alone. In other words, in life itself, and not actually in the goal proper, which it goes without saying cannot be anything except two times two makes four. That is, a formula. And after all, two times two makes four is already not life, gentlemen, but the beginning of death.

When we speak of how *A Course in Miracles* would look at this issue, we will see that the laws of this world really *are* laws of death, even though they seem so immutable and real.

7

At least man has always somehow feared this two times two makes four. And I fear it even now.

We fear it because it means our own death, the end of who we really are.

Possibly man does nothing but search for this two times two makes four, crosses oceans, gives his life in the search. But to find it, really to discover it, he is somehow afraid of that, so help me, God. After all, he senses that as soon as he finds it, there won't be anything left to search for.

As the workbook says, "The world I see holds nothing that I want" (W-pI.128), and when I finally get what I think I want in the world, I end up realizing it is nothing. This is what we are most afraid of, and it is what Dostoevsky is saying.

There's something uneasy about him, such a man, that can be observed when he has attained such goals. He likes the attaining, but not altogether to have attained, and that is, of course, terribly funny. In short, man is made in a comical way. But, two times two makes four is an insufferable thing. Two times two makes four is, in my opinion, nothing but an impertinence. Yes, sir. Two times two makes four looks like a dandy, struts like a cock of the walk, blocking your way, and spits.

In other words, it is really the world mocking us, which of course, is the ego in all of us mocking us by convincing us that its thought system of separation is reality, as is the world that arose from it along with its "natural" laws.

I agree that two times two makes four is a wonderful thing. But if we are to praise everything, then two times two makes five is sometimes a most delightful little thing.

The point of Dostoevsky's book is that two times two makes five *is* the wonderful thing. He understood the nature of the world, that there is no hope here, and that it is arrogant to think one can do something to correct the world's condition. That is why he eventually turned away from a political solution, even though, as we saw, he had been very attracted to it earlier in his life, and in fact wrote about it a great deal. He realized that political/social change was not the answer. Interestingly, by the way, in the last stage of his life he became a Christian, although he hated the Church, an attitude clearly depicted in the famous Grand Inquisitor scene in *The Brothers*

Karamazov. He believed that redemption lay only in accepting the love of Jesus within—not through the traditional Church that disgusted him with its hypocrisy. Dostoevsky was emphatic in his belief that the answer to humanity's problems lay not in the world, but rather in one's inner life. One does not get that from *Notes from Underground*, however.

And so Dostoevsky pokes fun at the attempts of contemporary Russians to make the world, and Russian society especially, a better place. He was saying that all those attempts deny the underground. (One can well see why Freud admired him so much.) They are all based in one way or another on a rationality that concludes that the way things are now is how things ought to be: two times two makes four. Real freedom, Dostoevsky believed, lay in denying that equation and recognizing that nothing here works. As *A Course in Miracles* would tell us, everything in this world lies; perception is a lie. "Nothing so blinding as perception of form" (T-22.III.6:7), and indeed, two times two equals five.

3. One True Equation

The only equation that works and represents the truth is (I am giving away the ending of the workshop): $1 + 1 = 1$. This is parallel to the idea given us by Jesus in the text: "a Oneness joined as One" (T-25.I.7:1); God plus Christ equals one Self. That is the only truth. The ego invented arithmetic, for God only knows *one*. There can be no arithmetic, let alone higher math or calculus, if there is only *one*. That is all God and His perfect Oneness knows. In the insanity of the separation, the ego said $1 + 1 = 2$, which means God and His Son equal two beings; and since there are two beings, they must be separate from each other. When we say $1 + 1 = 1$, however, which is Heaven's reality, there is no separation. As the workbook says, there is no place where the Father ends and the Son begins as something separate from Him. (W-pI.132.12:4). There are not two Beings in Heaven, God and Christ. There is just the perfect Oneness of God's perfect Love.

To the ego, there is God *and* His Son, Who becomes separate and distinct from His Creator and Source. Now there are two. That, of course, is the beginning of the separation, the beginning of the dream, the beginning of the *tiny, mad idea* taken seriously. The thought in everyone's mind is that there is God, there is me, and we are separate. And since I am now separate from God, the God I am separate from can no longer be the true God, my Creator and Source, because there is no separation in the true God. *Ideas do not leave their Source*: the Idea of God's Son (Christ) remains at one with Its Creator Source.

Yet, once we say $1 + 1 = 2$, we are talking about the separation, and the God we are separate from is the ego God. This is when the ego weaves its nightmarish myth of sin, guilt, and fear. It tells us that the God from Whom we have separated is on the warpath; His maniacal wrath is beyond all measure; and His only desire is to destroy us. The ego takes the mind's equation of $1 + 1 = 2$, projects it, makes up a world of separation, and it is in that world that we now have the law of $2 + 2 = 4$. This quickly expands to $4 + 4 = 8$, and we go on and on in all the different permutations and combinations of that original ego formula: $1 + 1 = 2$. This is the birth of arithmetic, higher mathematics, and all science; in fact it is the birth of everything. We end up in a world in which we have a body and brain that says $2 + 2 = 4$, a universe wherein there are laws to be followed regarding both the world and the body.

Later we will be considering Lesson 76, "I am under no laws but God's," probably one of the most misunderstood lessons in the workbook. There Jesus pokes fun at the so-called laws we follow about what is supposed to be and what is not supposed to be: the laws of relationships, medicine, health, money, and so on. This is also one of the places in *A Course in Miracles* where he talks about "stacks of green paper strips and piles of metal discs" that we think are so important (W-pI.76.3:2; see also T-27.VIII.2:2). He speaks as well about our belief that if we take a "small round pellet" or inject some fluid into our veins we "will ward off disease and death" (W-pI.76.3:3). Then there are the laws that define our relationship with God, which form the essence of what are known as formal religions. Thus there is a right and wrong way to look at the Deity, a right and wrong way to look at relationships, a right and wrong way to look at one's body. These are the kinds of things the underground man was railing against. While he was not necessarily a spokesman for everything Dostoevsky believed, he certainly was a spokesman for this aspect of Dostoevsky's thought: there is something radically wrong with the world and its thinking.

Dostoevsky was saying, and in a sense this is what Jesus wants us to understand, that while it is

13

important when living in this world to add up 2 and 2 and get 4—we could not survive here without being able to do that—it is even more important to know that $2 + 2 = 5$, acknowledging that the world and its laws are insane. The Lesson "I am under no laws but God's" often has its meaning distorted, sometimes with regrettable consequences, because students wrongly conclude that since Jesus says the laws we hold to be so sacred and inviolate are made up, it does not matter what we do. Thus, this "reasoning" goes, it is not necessary to go to doctors or to lock our doors; it does not matter what we eat, whom we sleep with, or what we do with God. We can do or not do what we want, because after all there are no laws here!

It was that lesson that first prompted me so many years ago to talk about Levels One and Two. In the years right after *A Course in Miracles* was published, I would speak a great deal about the confusion of levels. Level One has to do with the Course's metaphysical level: truth and illusion, reflected in Lesson 76. The law of love and oneness is the *only* law; all the rest are spurious. People, again, have taken that as license to do whatever they wish, to break every law because all laws are invalid, or to do the opposite and deny the body and world, becoming ascetic and sacrificial: since everything here is an illusion, and moreover the body is an expression of the mind's projected belief in sin, we should suffer and not enjoy ourselves. That is the very antithesis of what the Course teaches.

In Lesson 155, "I will step back and let Him lead the way," Jesus talks about the middle ground between the two extremes of (1) indulging yourself and breaking every law possible, thereby demonstrating that the world is an illusion; or (2) going in the opposite direction and shunning everything of the world because, as illusions, everything in it along with all thoughts and feelings about it are bad, in that they reinforce the belief that the separation is real. Thus, any degree of comfort is bad, whether derived from food, sex, having a nice car or home, etc. Between these two extremes there is a middle ground that rests on our understanding that to live in this world we have to add up 2 and 2 and get 4, but at the same time understand that if we want to awaken from this dream, we must realize that $2 + 2 = 5$, symbolizing our understanding that the world lies. We will return to this theme over and over throughout our discussion.

4. From the World to the Underground

In light of these ideas we can say that the purpose of our learning the world's laws and how to navigate them is so we can ultimately learn that $2 + 2 = 5$, without skipping over the step of first mastering the laws of the $2 + 2 = 4$ world. We will end up not breaking the laws, but simply not giving them any power over us. That is the difference. We do not break the laws as proof that the laws are insane, which would merely be a form of adolescent rebellion. Instead, we learn how to live within the laws, not because they are wonderful and are true, but because we are here in a body and the body is our classroom.

One of the most important lessons in this classroom of being in the physical world is learning how not to be affected by the body or its world. We live as if $2 + 2 = 4$, while knowing in our hearts that the real answer is 5. This, then, becomes the stepping-stone to the ultimate equation: $1 + 1 = 1$. But we cannot get to that until we first learn how to add 2 and 2 and get 4, recognizing everything that equation represents.

We made the body as a limitation on love (T-18. VIII.1) and the world as an attack on God's Love (W-pII.3.2:1). Both the world and body, therefore,

were made to exclude love. One of the key ideas in
A Course in Miracles is that once we believe we are
bodies living in the world (originally a symbol of
sin), they become neutral (W-pII.294). As neutral, the
body is seen as a classroom in which we can learn one
of two lessons from one of two teachers: from the ego
we learn how to make other people responsible for
the separation that has been accepted as real, whereas
from Jesus we learn that the world is a classroom in
which we will come to perceive the world as illusory.
The body is neither good or bad; the world is neither
good or bad. They are simply classrooms in which we
learn to get from the world back to the mind. To use
Dostoevsky's terms, we learn to get from the world to
the underground, while in Freudian language we learn
to get from the world to the unconscious ego, which
the Course teaches is the mind's defense against the
unconscious Love of the Holy Spirit (the Atonement
principle).

The world, then, becomes something for which we
are grateful, because once we are here and trapped
in the thought system of the ego, there is no way out
until we choose a new teacher. That new teacher helps
us realize that the world is not the problem, nor its law
that $2 + 2 = 4$. In this sense, Dostoevsky did not go far
enough. The real problem is that we have denied the

ego's foundational law, which is that $1 + 1 = 2$. It is not the world's laws that are the problem, but our belief in the fundamental law that the separation is true: There is God and there is the Son, and They are different: two separated entities. That is the problem. But if we keep attacking, denying, and becoming upset about $2 + 2$ equaling 4, we will never get beyond that level to the fact that it is a projection of $1 + 1 = 2$. In this sense the world becomes a very important part of our journey home. To borrow Freud's famous term, the world is the *royal road* that leads out of hell and back to Heaven.

Dostoevsky was at least partly right in recognizing that attempting to fix the world is the wrong focus. What are we fixing? We are attempting to fix something that does not exist, something that is not the problem. Dostoevsky, of course, did not say that, but he did say that we deny who we are as a person when we focus on the world, when we believe we are actually accomplishing something by building "a crystal palace." This referred to a crystal palace in England that had come to symbolize this new way of thinking, of making something beautiful and wonderful in the world. Once we do that, Dostoevsky held, we deny the essence of who we are.

Restating this in terms of *A Course in Miracles*, we would say that by focusing on the world we are hiding our unconscious decision to deny the mind. Our identity as minds is what we really fear since they contain the power to undo the ego, simply by our withdrawing all belief in it. We are not afraid of $2 + 2$ being 4; we are afraid of $1 + 1$ being 2, and we are afraid of that because it is our defense against what we are even more afraid of: $1 + 1 = 1$; i.e., the separation never happened. Choosing that is our ego's real fear.

The ego cleverly builds layers of defenses to keep this underlying fear hidden. It is afraid of the Holy Spirit's Atonement thought—more specifically, of our choosing to identify with the Holy Spirit's Atonement thought. This is the thought that says regardless of what we are dreaming, one plus one still equals one— the separation never happened. That is at the bottom of our topographical mind. The layer atop that is the ego's claim that $1+1$ is not 1, but 2. There is God and there is the "I," the separated self; there is God, the object of our sin, and there is the "I" that is guilty over the sin and fears punishment. We project that, so God now becomes the sinner. First He was sinned against, but now He is the sinner Who will destroy us. This is the ego's world of $1 + 1 = 2$.

While this is totally insane, it becomes the source of terror for all of us, what we flee from. We therefore make up a world in which we have a multitude of laws: science, mathematics, religion, economics, and relationships—the body's laws that enunciate what is supposed to be and what is not supposed to be. Yet they are nothing but subterfuges so that we will never get back to what the ego says is the real problem: the thought that we are separate, that $1 + 1 = 2$. As long as we are afraid of facing that, we will be attracted to the world, and one of the ways of maintaining this attraction is to focus on fixing the world. Once again, this is what Dostoevsky recognized very early in his life: nothing is remedied by trying to fix the world and society.

I have occasionally commented on a statement Freud made in 1930 about socialism and Marxism—about 70 years after Dostoevsky's story about the underground man. Freud said that these systems would fail. While he did not consider himself a Marxist, he was favorably disposed toward the ideal of alleviating people's suffering, both physical and economic. Yet he said these kinds of systems would fail because they did not take into account man's innate aggressiveness (exactly what Dostoevsky said), as well as their special relationships (the Course's term):

> But it cannot be assumed that economic motives
> are the only ones that determine the behavior
> of human beings in society.... It is altogether
> incomprehensible how psychological factors can
> be overlooked where what is in question are the
> reactions of living human beings; for not only
> were these reactions concerned in establishing
> the economic conditions, but even under the
> domination of those conditions men can only bring
> the original instinctual impulses into play—their
> self-preservative instinct, their aggressiveness,
> their need to be loved, their drive towards
> obtaining pleasure and avoiding unpleasure.*

When you try to fix things in the world you deny
the underground. You deny that in the unconscious, as
Freud might say, $2 + 2 = 5$. Freud always emphasized
that the unconscious is irrational and does not obey
the world's laws. Very strange things happen at the
unconscious level. We have glimpses of this in our
dreams at night, where things happen that are not
natural, things that could not happen in what we
think of as the real world. People change shapes; two
characters are fused into one; people fly and do all

---

* *New Introductory Lectures on Psychoanalysis* in *The Standard
Edition of the Complete Psychological Works of Sigmund Freud.*
Hogarth Press. London: 1960, p. 178.

sorts of out-of-the-ordinary things. They represent our unconscious thoughts and symbols being thrown up into awareness, at least nocturnal awareness.

Freud's point was that fixing things in the world will make no difference and therefore make no sense if you do not deal with the underlying cause. And, of course, that is Jesus' point in *A Course in Miracles*. No matter how well-meaning you are, no matter how spiritually advanced your utopian vision may appear to be, it will fail if it does not have built into it some means of confronting this underground, this unconscious reservoir of hate, greed, selfishness, and guilt. If that is not looked at, exposed, and chosen against, nothing will ever change because these unconscious thoughts are continually projected out, albeit in disguised form. The give-away is, to go back to Dostoevsky, that the world and all of our visions are based on $2 + 2$ equaling 4, when the reflected reality within the dream is that $2 + 2 = 5$. In other words, the world lies, and so we should not believe anything anyone says here. Trust no one who comes from the perspective of the world and is reflecting the laws of the world.

Nonetheless, as teachers of children, we certainly want to teach them the world's laws. As parents, we want to teach our children how to function here, as illusory as it might be. But if we do not come from a position of love, which is reflected here by 2 + 2 equaling 5, we will be teaching our children how to cut off their only means of salvation and hope. We will end up teaching them how to become world machines, like everyone else. We certainly want to help our children function effectively in the world, *but for a different purpose*. And we do this by instructing them with love instead of specialness, separation, and guilt.

Thus, while we teach our children—as teachers, relatives, or any other role—deep down we realize that it does not matter what they do or become in this world as long as they do it selflessly. If we come from a position of selfless love ourselves, that is what we will be teaching them, and that is what they will really learn. It does not matter what our children do in the world, because if all they learn is to become master mathematicians, thereby always adding up 2 + 2 and getting 4, they are going to end up dead. This was Dostoevsky's message: 2 times 2 equaling 4 equals death. It is the death of our right mind, where 2 + 2 = 5. This is why it makes no sense to ask Jesus or the Holy Spirit to help us in this world, to help us do arithmetic. The only way They will help us do arithmetic will result in our failing our exam! So do not ask Them to help you with that. Ask instead that They help you not take seriously your learning that $2 + 2 = 4$.

We need to walk a fine line as adults in this world. We have a responsibility to our children, but the responsibility is not on the level of form but on the level of content, an expression of the true teaching and learning that $2 + 2 = 5$. By not getting upset when children make a mistake or do something wrong or disobey us, we are teaching them that, yes, it is important to learn that $2 + 2 = 4$, but in reality $2 + 2 = 5$. That does not mean we should not be firm with them or not correct their mistakes. It means that when we get personally upset over something they do wrong or something the president, prime minister, or congress does wrong, we are saying: "Don't you know that two and two does not equal five? It equals four! What you are doing is ruining everything." Well, how could someone ruin everything when there is nothing here to ruin? This means that if we get personally upset and our peace is disrupted, we are saying it *does* matter, and that we want $2 + 2$ to be 4. The point is that $2 + 2 = 5$. Perception lies! "Nothing so blinding as perception of form," to quote that incisive line again. The world lies. The only reason we believe $2 + 2 = 4$ is that we are terrified of the guilt over believing 1 + 1 = 2, and we are terrified because we are really afraid of the fact that 1 + 1 = 1.

Jesus tells us in Chapter 13, "You are not really afraid of crucifixion. Your real terror is of redemption" (T-13.III.1:10-11). He is saying that we are not afraid that 1 + 1 = 2, that God will crucify us because of what we have done. Our fear is that 1 + 1 has *always* been 1. Accepting this happy truth is our redemption. We get so far away from that, though, when we become involved with proving that 2 + 2 = 4, when we are sure we know what is going on and why, certain that people are wrong in how they do things. To be sure, people do things wrong in the world, but the whole world is wrong! Yet when we insist that people are doing bad things in the world and that we have a better way of doing them, we are just as insane as they, which is why nothing ever changes. No social or political movement, no revolution or rebellion has ever really worked, because none of them has aimed at changing people's minds. That does not mean there should not be attempts to improve situations in the world, nor that we should not join movements to bring about such improvements. We just need to realize that if we do not join the movement out of love, realizing that love here is the reflection of the Oneness of God and the Sonship, we are part of the problem.

26

It is essential to understand that I am not talking about behavior, nor is *A Course in Miracles*. None of what I am saying should be taken to mean that you should not be involved in the world and attempt to make things better here. It is fine to work toward having $2 + 2 = 4$ and to teach people that, as long as you know in your heart of hearts that it is really 5. This will help you not take anything here seriously. You cannot help anyone—a loved one or groups in the world—if you take their suffering seriously. This is the ego's plan, that we take things here seriously. $1 + 1$ equaling 2 is a very serious equation, and everything following that shares in its seriousness.

If you really want to be of help in this world, remember that $2 + 2 = 5$. Things are not what they appear to be, as Plato taught two and a half millennia ago. Everything in this world is a lie as long as it is taken seriously, which does not mean you cavalierly dismiss or become insensitive to people's suffering. You simply redefine the suffering. *Everyone* suffers who thinks $2 + 2 = 4$, because that is a lie, denying the reality of God and His Son. Moreover, we made up bodies and brains to perpetuate the lie, which is a projection of the real problem that $1 + 1 = 2$. And actually even that is not the problem, as I have been saying. The problem is we chose to believe that

= 2. The "we" is the decision maker, the part ⌐ minds that decided that $1 + 1 = 2$ instead of believing the Holy Spirit Who said, "No, one and one have always equaled one, and will only do so." Thus, the problem is that our minds chose the wrong teacher of arithmetic.

We can see how far removed we get when we try to correct things in the world, thinking we are actually correcting them. One more time, I am not saying not to correct things in the world. We would be remiss as parents and teachers if we did not correct children who do not know how to get 4 when they add 2 and 2. They cannot get to 5 until they first learn the world's arithmetic and how to function normally. Only then can we teach them that $2 + 2$ is really 5. So often the most loving thing is to correct errors on the level of form. As citizens of this country and of the world, for example, often the most right-minded thing we can do is to correct the mistakes that have been made in our name, *as long as we do not take any of it seriously*. And how do you know when you have done so? When you get angry, when you see the person or groups of people you are blaming for the world's inequities as truly different from you. Then you know you have fallen back into the ego's trap of taking the *tiny, mad idea* seriously and making it real.

28

5. From the Underground to the Truth

The snares of specialness are ever so devious and insidious, often masquerading as holiness. And the height of special love is spiritual specialness. We know we have fallen into the ego's web of specialness when we make the differences among us real. There certainly are differences on the level of the body, but they are all superficial. What is not superficial is the inherent sameness of all of us as minds. Take those considered to be the most wicked and evil people in the world, the light of Christ still shines in them, and they are as afraid of that light as we all are. We know we are afraid because we are attacking them, not liking the way they do arithmetic. It simply boils down to our believing that we have a better way of doing arithmetic! But arithmetic lies.

The only number that is true is 1, and the reflection of Heaven's Oneness in this world is that we are all the same. We are not asked in this course to get back to the Oneness of God, or even to understand this Oneness. Jesus makes that quite clear in the first section in Chapter 25 when he tells us that we are not asked to understand how "a Oneness joined as One" is true (T-25.I.7:1). All we are asked is to seek his help to learn how to live the reflection of that Oneness here. Our sameness is on the level of the mind, and consists of the same ego, the same Holy Spirit, and the same power to choose between them. This is in *everyone*. If we make one exception, we have crucified Christ and His Wholeness once again. Indeed, Christ can be defined by His wholeness, His undivided Oneness. If we exclude one person, we are saying Christ is no longer whole. This is His true crucifixion, which happened right at the beginning when we said $1 + 1 = 2$. We relive this over and over and over in every twinge of judgment, let alone every expression of hate. Every time we judge and make someone wrong we are again crucifying God's Son, and the only reason we do this is that we do not want to be part of His Oneness. Our thinking then evolves into: "*I* am not the one who crucified Christ; *you* are. Yes, I attacked you. Sure, I don't like you. But I had no choice. Look what you did to me." This is the "face of innocence" that Jesus describes near the end of the text (see T-31.V), which ensures that the duality of the ego's world will continue to reign supreme.

There is no hope in this world if you think there is a world to save. As Jesus tells us in Lesson 132, "There is no world! This is the central thought the course attempts to teach" (W-pI.132.6:2-3). Why

30

bother, then, trying to save it? It is so important to realize we are talking about an attitude, not about behavior or about the body doing something. You use your activities in the world as a way of teaching everyone that $2 + 2 = 5$, and you do this on a practical level by not letting the world get to you, by not giving the world power over you, by not letting people's mistakes and sins affect you, by not letting the atrocities people commit in the name of God, truth, and freedom affect you. If they do make you angry, disgusted, or despairing, you are saying $2 + 2 = 4$. *That and only that is the problem.*

And so, if you believe reality is that $2 + 2 = 4$, you will never grow into being able to say it is 5. This means you will never be able to look at what underlies it, which is that $1 + 1$ equaling 2 is an illusion. If the world is an illusion in which $2 + 2 = 4$ and not 5, then the mind that says $1 + 1 = 2$ is also an illusion. The simple truth is that $1 + 1 = 1$. We get very far away from that when we find ourselves in a world and body trying to do something about them.

The ego is clever and sly and has pulled the wool over almost everyone's eyes. Whether you think the world is a wonderful or hateful place, you think it is a place. That is the problem. The ego has you, and does not care at that point whether you are a saint or

31

a sinner, whether the world adores or reviles you. You think it is a place and therefore think that what you do here means something and is important. There are even some very strange people who think this blue book is important. How could a bunch of nothing be important? What is important is what *A Course in Miracles* reflects, but not the Course itself as a book that contains lots of words.

What is wrong with the world is not what goes on in the world. There is no world! How could anything go on in a place that does not exist? What is wrong with the world is the thought system the world expresses. It is the thought system that you want to change, and the way you change it is to look at its fundamental premise, $1 + 1 = 2$, and gently smile. As Jesus tells us, "It is a joke to think that time can come to circumvent eternity, which *means* there is no time" (T-27.VIII.6:5). Eternity is $1 + 1 = 1$. Time is $1 + 1 = 2$, and in form it is $2 + 2 = 4$. It is a joke to think that they really do.

We need but look at $1 + 1 = 2$ and say, "What did I get so hot and bothered about? Why go to all the trouble of making a world to hide from that? This is absolutely ludicrous. God has not been compromised. His Son has not been crucified. Nothing has changed." We learn this lesson and exemplify it by not letting anything in this insane world take away the experience of love and peace within us. We do not let anything others do or say affect the love we have for them. We do not have to get hifalutin with the metaphysics of the Course. We need only recognize that any time our peace is disturbed it is not for the reason we think, as the early lesson says (W-pI.5). That makes these teachings practical, specific, and easy to practice. It is not always easy to do, but the basic principle is very simple. Just be vigilant: watch yourself when you get upset, depressed, angry, guilty, or anxious; when you plot vengeance; when you start fantasizing; when any of your thoughts on any level serve to separate you from someone else; when your thoughts serve to make your body or someone else's body real; when they make the world real, or when they seem to suggest there is a problem out there that has to be addressed.

Whenever you experience any of these feelings or thoughts, you know you have listened to the wrong teacher and have looked at the *tiny, mad idea* and its forms of expression and remembered not to laugh at them. Indeed, one of the most important sentences in the Course is: "Into eternity, where all is one, there crept a tiny, mad idea, at which the Son of God remembered not to laugh" (T-27.VIII.6:2). The world is nothing more than a projection of that *tiny, mad idea* that was taken seriously. The seriousness is the problem. We know that as we live our lives, serious things happen. Taking care of our own body and the bodies of loved ones is serious business. Living in a world where bodies do unconscionably cruel, merciless, and vicious things is serious. The lesson is that we not be tempted by the ego's urgings to take it seriously. How could God's Son separate from Him? That is absurd. How could perfect Oneness be shattered? Yet, those are the thoughts that underlie everything in the phenomenal universe.

A Course in Miracles offers us a perspective from which to understand what our lives are about, what goes on in our bodies with our thoughts and feelings, what goes on in other people's bodies. We have a context for looking at all that now and seeing it differently. What the world says is true and right and moral is insane. What it says is healthy and not healthy, appropriate and not appropriate is insane. That does not mean that you do not act appropriately in the roles you have chosen as your classrooms, but it does mean that you do not take it seriously when you do. You learn that $2 + 2 = 4$ so you can get beyond it to learn that $2 + 2$ really equals 5. This allows you to move from the world to the mind where you have a chance to look at the underlying equation that started the trouble in the first place: $1 + 1 = 2$.

To repeat this important clarification, I am not saying people should be inappropriate, that they should glorify pathology, or that it is okay for people to do cruel and terrible things. I am simply saying that we should obey the laws of the world *because* they are silly, a vehicle for expressing the Atonement principle that love has not been affected by thoughts of sin and judgment. Nonetheless, sometimes it is helpful not to obey the laws, not out of a spirit of rebellion or revolution, but because love has guided us that way. Always remember that *love is oneness*. Even if we lead a political revolt, we can do so lovingly if we do not make the people we are rebelling against the bad guys. If we do, our revolt will be just as bad as the tyranny we are trying to change. We need merely look at the French Revolution as an example: the storming of the Bastille led to the Reign of Terror and ended with Napoleon. And our recent history has provided many other examples of seemingly well-intentioned people or governments gone awry with hate. If we do anything in a spirit of opposition, we become part of the problem, which is why nothing ever changes in a significant way. That was Freud's brilliant point: any utopian vision will fail if it does not take into account man's innate aggressiveness—guilt and hate. These are ignored only at our own peril.

You have to go into the underground, not because it is real, but because that is where the problem is. Only then can you choose against it. Do not be taken in by what goes on in the world. I cannot say it often enough, and as you know, Jesus says it over and over: *the world is insane*. You could be a dedicated and sincere student of this course and still somehow get caught up in the insanity of the world and, not realizing its insanity, think it means something— for example, that it needs to be saved. The truly healed person is able to live in this world and live like other people, but not take any of it seriously. The beginning of Lesson 155 says the healed person looks like everyone else, dresses, eats, and talks like everyone else, but "smile[s] more frequently" (W-pI.155.1:2). You smile more frequently because you know $2 + 2 = 5$. You smile at those who swear that $2 + 2 = 4$, and that their version of arithmetic is better than others'. Such madness is not sinful, evil, or wicked. It is plain silly. But you know this only when you truly know that nothing here works, and nothing here means anything. $2 + 2 = 5$.

To repeat, *Nothing so blinding as perception of form*. In the world of form, $2 + 2 = 4$. There are laws and causal connections that are upheld within the dream, but in your right mind you know that your reality is outside the dream. This happy dream is $2 + 2 = 5$. Jesus tells us that of all the many causes of our suffering, we did not think our guilt was among them (T-27.VII.7:4). The world says suffering comes from X, Y, and Z: $2 + 2 = 4$. Jesus says, no, suffering comes from our guilt: $2 + 2 = 5$. The world does not know how to add! It not only thinks it does, but unfortunately is certain it does.

6. Questions

Q: You said you could revolt, but implicit in the word *revolt* is *against*. How do you go to war and right-mindedly knock people off?

A: No, you go to war and you do not knock people off. You can go to war and know you are not in the dream. That is an extreme example, to be sure; but you do it because, in a sense, that is the classroom you are in for whatever reason. Most people would agree that lovingly telling a white lie to a little child is appropriate, while killing people with an Uzi machine gun would not be. Yet they seem different only because people think the body is real and that there is a hierarchy of illusions. When you tell a white lie to a child or to anyone else, the intention can be loving. Why can't you go to war and still have the intention of being loving? In principle, you could shoot a gun without doing it in a spirit of anger or glee. *But*—you can go to war right-mindedly only when your mind is healed.

Generally speaking, we cannot avoid killing living things in our world. The idea is not to do it out of hate or fear. There is no right or wrong way, but it is possible to live one's life without intentionally trying to hurt anyone or anything. It is also possible that a person could be in a right-minded state and not kill a spider, for instance, or be in a right-minded state and kill it. There is no right or wrong behavior, only right- and wrong-minded thoughts. What makes *A Course in Miracles* so difficult is that it is totally radical. *Radical* means "root," going to the root of something. The root of the ego's world is $1 + 1 = 2$, manifested by seeing yourself as separate from someone, whether it is a spider, an enemy on a battlefield, or a person you live or work with. That misperception is the problem. What you do behaviorally once you realize that $1 + 1 = 1$ does not matter. You just want to be clear that you do not believe $1 + 1 = 2$.

There is something amiss, though, if you feel guilty about killing a spider, but you do not feel guilty about killing a person psychologically—family, friend, or public figure. People often have issues around this. I remember someone at our Center in New York talking about how upset he got when he saw someone killing bugs, because the bugs were living things to him. He had no compunction at all, though, about judging or using others for his own needs. This shows that something is not right, because if you truly care about the spider, you will also care about everything else you think is alive—animal and vegetable—no matter where it is on the so-called chain of being. Making distinctions shows that something is wrong in what you are doing. This is helpful information to have, because very often strong feelings about not killing a spider are accompanied by anger toward people who do kill them. It is difficult to take a position like that without somehow judging people who do not practice what you do. Thus you are saying that there is something holy about a spider, but not so holy about a person who kills them. And so the Sonship has been fragmented and the Wholeness of Christ destroyed.

There are many other examples: your car does not work and you slam it; you are a baseball player and strike out, then go back to the dugout and kick the water fountain; your boss reprimands you and you go home and are mean to the dog. In all these examples, the issue is not whether what you are attacking is alive or not, or higher or lower on the evolutionary chain. What matters is what is inside you, and that you are projecting your own guilt in the form of anger. People always judge behavior, which is why they believe that $2 + 2 = 4$. What unifies everything is what is going on in the mind. Kicking a car, a water fountain, an animal, a radio that does not work, or attacking a person—all of these are the same. They come from the projection of guilt, and the mind's decision for guilt is the only issue.

Often what people do—this is an example of *reaction formation,* where you deny what is in your mind by behaviorally doing the opposite—is announce that they will never kill certain living things, but if that does not generalize to everyone and everything, then what they are really doing is trying magically to contain their self-hatred and murderous tendencies. This is no different from people who always have to be in control and have everything in their outer world be just right. They are reacting to their being out of control within. Any time you have an investment in something external, it is a reaction to the opposite inside. *Reaction formation* is a psychological rule with no exceptions. Whenever you are invested in things being a certain way, thinking it is important to do or not to do, you are affirming that $2 + 2 = 4$. And this is a reaction to your belief that $1 + 1 = 2$. You are overwhelmed with guilt over the thought that led to that: I destroyed, betrayed, rejected, and abandoned love, which resulted in $1 + 1 = 1$ changing to $1 + 1 = 2$. Your guilt over this perceived sin is so enormous that you now try to hide from it, proclaiming that you are not like that at all. Indeed, you love everything and everyone. But you do not! You just love certain things and certain people. Again, when you strong need not to kill, or not to behave in a ____ way, it is only because you are trying to hold in check the unconscious need to do the opposite, magically hoping to avoid punishment over your perceived sin of rejecting love.

This is not to say that discipline is a bad thing, but it will not solve the real problem. Acting on the magical idea that by controlling things outside you are controlling things inside never works. What is inside remains inside, and what remains unconscious automatically and inevitably will be projected. So you will always be fighting against this hate inside. That is why it is wise to avoid religious fanatics—to cite one form this dynamic takes—because their protestations of love and arguing for the truth of their religion is a defense against their believing just the opposite (again, *reaction formation*). The hate inside always needs an outlet, which is why zealots are filled with judgment. Indeed, fanatics on any level—political, religious, social—are projecting outside what they do not want to look at inside.

If you are right-minded and live in a world of $2 + 2 = 4$, you do not get upset because you know $2 + 2 = 5$. Therefore you give nothing in this world power to take away the certainty of that love, the certainty of knowing that nothing here means anything. Without guilt and its projections, nothing interferes with the flow of love from your mind. Thus you are kind to everyone, and this is so whether or not you kill a spider, eat a cow, or drop a bomb.

The point here is that we want to use our body's thoughts and feelings to return to the mind. Once again, there is nothing right or wrong about behavior. In this world, after all, we have to do something with our bodies. We all have needs, likes, dislikes, and so on. However, we do not have to give them power to affect our peace or separate us from our brothers. The idea is not to judge our thoughts or behavior, or to judge others for theirs.

Q: On Monday nights I like to play poker with friends. And I always feel guilty when I'm done because I think I shouldn't be doing that. My heart races at the end, and whether I should go or not becomes an obsession.

A: That's exactly what the ego wants, for then it becomes: to play poker or not to play poker, that is the question. That's a little silly, right? What kind of question is that? Do you think Jesus really cares if you play poker or not? He would be a lousy poker player anyway, because a winning hand to him would be *one* of a kind.

Playing poker in and of itself does not matter. What matters is going there peacefully; and while you are playing, being peaceful; and when you return home, being peaceful. The issue is not poker or no poker. We all fall into that trap. Do I do this? Do I not? Implicit in what you are saying is that poker is not a spiritual activity, and therefore you think that instead of playing poker you should be studying the Course, or listening to some profound CD, or meditating on the eternal verities, or doing something you think is spiritual. But you could have just as holy an instant playing poker with the guys as you could doing anything else. The lesson for you is that you can play poker, have a good time, and not make a big deal about it. If you win, you win; if you lose, you lose, but it is a pleasant few hours with people you like and do not judge. Poker, then, becomes a classroom for learning not to give the world power. The ego has us believe there is a hierarchy of illusions, with poker being low on the scale and those who play even lower. But how can that be if there is no hierarchy? Only the content of love is true in the world of illusion.

Q: There is a very sweet movie about penguins, and everyone gets upset about this one scene where the raven attacks a baby penguin, but no one says anything about the scene where the penguins eat the fish.

A: Of course, and no one really thinks of the poor raven. I mean, that is what ravens do; penguins get eaten and they also eat; and there are other birds that prey on ravens. That is what life is: *one or the other* (*kill or be killed*). It is what we can think of as cannibalism: feeding off something external to fulfill our needs. Everyone makes distinctions in a world where $2 + 2 = 4$. We say there are versions of this equation that are better than others. For example, some animals are sweet and innocent and can be excused for their cannibalism, while others are awful and mean. *Everyone* here is awful and mean, because it was an awful and mean thought that got us here in the first place.

7. The Laws of God and the World

"Perception and Choice"

As an introduction to our study of Lesson 76, "I am under no laws but God's," let us look at some passages that make the distinction between the laws of God and the laws of the world, and that also state that God does not know about this world and our perceptions. We begin with a selection from "Perception and Choice" in Chapter 25:

(T-25.III.2:1) God's laws do not obtain directly to a world perception rules, for such a world could not have been created by the Mind to which perception has no meaning.

This is just one among dozens and dozens of places where it is clear that *A Course in Miracles* is teaching that God did not create the world; in fact, God does not even know of this world since it does not exist. And so God's laws—derived from one plus one equals one—have nothing to do with this perceptual world. The law of perception is $1 + 1 = 2$; projected into the world it is $2 + 2 = 4$, along with all the other laws here.

(T-25.III.2:2) Yet are His laws reflected everywhere.

God's law is the law of perfect Oneness, eternity, and Love. The law of perfect Oneness is reflected here in the world in our seeing everyone as the same. We are all very different on the level of form, but on the level of the mind we are the same: we all have a wrong mind, a right mind, and a decision maker.

(T-25.III.2:3-5) Not that the world where this reflection is, is real at all. Only because His Son believes it is, and from His Son's belief He could not let Himself be separate entirely. He could not enter His Son's insanity with him, but He could be sure His sanity went there with him, so he could not be lost forever in the madness of his wish.

This is an anthropomorphic way of saying that when we fell asleep, we took with us into our dream a memory of Who we really are, a thought that reminds us that the separation never happened. That memory or thought is what *A Course in Miracles* calls the Holy Spirit. In truth, God did not do anything. He did not create the Holy Spirit; He did not give an answer to the separation because there was no separation. The principle of the Atonement is that the separation never happened, and we forever remain as God created us, at one with Him. Accordingly, when *A Course in Miracles* speaks of the Holy Spirit as a Voice, it is telling us that this is the Voice that reminds us—not really in words, but as the perceived presence of our own right-minded thought—that we have never left home.

"There Is No Love but God's"

We now turn to two paragraphs in Lesson 127, "There is no love but God's," which make very clear that God's laws can have no direct expression in this world.

(W-pI.127.3:1-3) Love cannot judge. As it is one itself, it looks on all as one. Its meaning lies in oneness.

In these last two sentences we have three *ones*: *one*, *one,* and *oneness*—the nature of love. We reflect that oneness here by abandoning judgment and perceiving everyone as sharing the same nightmare dream, the same need to awaken from this dream, and the same power to make the right choice. Thus, God is not here, His Love is not here, but the memory of that Love is. It takes the form of our recognizing the inherent sameness of God's Son: in Heaven we are one in Christ as spirit, while in the illusion we are one in the split mind. This is what unifies us.

(W-pI.127.3:4) And it [oneness] **must elude the mind that thinks of it as partial or in part.**

Note the clever word play on the word *partial*. *Partial* means that one is biased for or against something. A little later in the workbook, Jesus engages in the same word play (W-pI.161.2:4). *Partial* also means "part," as in "separate." As long as we think of ourselves as separate and as partial—people we like and people we do not like—we can never know oneness. This is why we can never understand Heaven and will always remain partial to the ego.

(W-pI.127.3:5-7) There is no love but God's, and all of love is His. There is no other principle that rules where love is not. Love is a law without an opposite.

In this world love has an opposite. For instance, I loved you yesterday; I do not love you today. I love this one; I do not love that one. Once love is reduced to a body, it has to be separate. We can say that the opposite of love in this world is fear or hate. But true love has no opposite because it is non-dualistic, being only one. Where love does not exist, nothing else does either. That is why there is nothing in this world; why, indeed, there is no world.

(W-pI.127.3:7-8) Love is a law without an opposite. Its wholeness is the power holding everything as one, the link between the Father and the Son which holds Them both forever as the same.

In Heaven, there is not a Father and a Son, God and Christ, Creator and created. That is dualism. If They are the same and They are one, there is no place, as quoted earlier, where one ends and the other begins (W-pI.132.12:4). It is only on this side of the veil, within the dream, that we conceive of Heaven as dualistic: God *and* His Son.

Again, what reflects that law of love in this world is the practice of forgiveness, which sees that the differences that appear to keep us separate and differentiated from each other are illusory because perception lies. $2 + 2$ does not equal 4. It does within the dream, just as hate and specialness seem real and justified here. Bodily needs, physical and psychological, are palpably present in the dream. But perception lies, as do bodies, because they come from the thought that is itself a lie: $1 + 1 = 2$—God and His Son are not the same and are not perfectly one. That is the reason the world was made as an attack on God (W-pII.3.2:1). $1 + 1 = 2$ is an attack on God, saying perfect Oneness is no longer perfect Oneness.

Now we skip to paragraph 5.

(W-pI.127.5:1-2) No law the world obeys can help you grasp love's meaning. What the world believes was made to hide love's meaning, and to keep it dark and secret.

Believing that $2 + 2 = 4$ will not teach you what reality is. While it will teach you how the world works and help you get along in it, it will not get you beyond it. But understanding that $2 + 2 = 5$ will help you see the world as an illusion because it helps you realize the world lies to protect its source in the wrong mind.

Love's meaning is oneness, which is not possible in the world of bodies because they separate. The laws of relationships result in separation. Moreover, there is *a hierarchy of illusions* here. It is acceptable to kill some insects but not others. It is acceptable to kill some animals and vegetables but not others. It is acceptable to hate or kill some people but not others. This belief in levels of differences is the ego's first law of chaos (see T-23.II.2), and its inherent inequality is how you know the entire world is built on a lie.

Do not trust anything people tell you here, unless they truly know that $2 + 2 = 5$. Only then should you believe them. Why do you want to trust those who have deceived themselves? The laws of science lie. Every law in this world lies. The one thing here that does not lie is the reflection of the law of love, the reflection of oneness: the vision of the sameness of God's Sons. That is the only truth within the lie, because that is the truth that leads us beyond the lie. The world's belief that $2 + 2 = 4$, that separation is real, "was made to hide love's meaning, and to keep it dark and secret." Love's meaning is that we are one: $1 + 1 = 1$. The world was made to hide this fact; hidden first by $1 + 1 = 2$, the ego thought system that is then projected out as a world where $2 + 2 = 4$. The world and our experiences here become the ego's sublime defense.

(W-pI.127.5:3) There is not one principle the world upholds but violates the truth of what love is, and what you are as well.

That is a very clear and strong statement. "There is not one principle the world upholds but violates the truth of what love is," which means every principle in this world violates love because they all make separation and the world real. The world has laws with seemingly logical, causal connections, yet it is all one colossal hoax, part of the ego's conspiracy to keep us mindless in the world.

It cannot be emphasized too often that this does not mean we should not learn how to live in the world. We have to do that, but we can never learn from the world if we are always fighting against it. As Lesson 184 explains, we can learn the world's symbols and function in accord with them, not because we believe them, but because the world is the classroom in which we learn and teach. The various symbols of our lives become the classrooms through which this learning and teaching occur, the truth beyond the symbols teaching through us. We need to learn the symbols of the world in which $2 + 2 = 4$, at the same time knowing it is really 5.

To repeat: "There is not one principle the world upholds but violates the truth of what love is, and what you are as well." What are you? You are God's Son as He created you, which means you are perfectly unified and integrated within your Self, and one with the Sonship because Christ is One. From a right-minded perspective, within the ego's dream of God's Son, we are one in possessing the same split mind and in sharing the same purpose. At the beginning of the teachers' manual Jesus states that the primary characteristic of a teacher of God is that he no longer sees another's interests as separate from his own. (M-1.1:1-2). Good guys and bad guys, victimizers and victims, torturers and tortured—all have the same split mind, including the single need to awaken from this dream and go home.

8. "I Am Under No Laws but God's"

As I mentioned earlier, this lesson, along with a number of other passages in *A Course in Miracles*, originally led me to talk about Levels One and Two. Within months of the Course's publication, it became apparent that students were already thinking that since the world is an illusion, it did not matter what anyone did. I therefore tried to help people realize that the Course is written on two levels. There are the either-or statements such as those found in this lesson: God's laws and the world's laws, with nothing in between. This first level, the foundation of the Course's non-dualistic metaphysics, contrasts truth and illusion without compromise: one is real, the other is not.

These principles, however, do not provide practical help in living in a world within which we all identify as bodies. And so the level *A Course in Miracles* is written on most of the time is what I call Level Two. This level deals only with illusion, and it is on this level that we find the contrast between the Holy Spirit's way of looking and the ego's. *Both are illusory*. The difference is that the ego's illusions keep us rooted in the dream, whereas the Holy Spirit's illusion—forgiveness—helps us awaken from it.

Since the potential for confusing these two levels is particularly great in this lesson, we look at some of its key ideas, beginning with the first paragraph.

(W-pI.76.1:1) We have observed before how many senseless things have seemed to you to be salvation.

Jesus refers to our special relationships, everything we think makes us feel good. There are laws here to that effect. For example, to take the most basic: If I am hungry, the law is that if I eat, I will feel better, and of course we all have our individual ways of expressing that need: if I eat certain foods I will feel sick, but if I eat other foods I will feel good. This law definitely works within the world of $2 + 2 = 4$. Just as we will not be able to get very far in this world if we cannot add $2 + 2$, we also will not get very far if we do not know how to eat. The same is the case with oxygen. If we do not get enough in our lungs, we will not survive.

While these laws keep the body alive, we do not have to see them as our salvation. We know some people live to eat. Indeed, we all have to eat to survive, but almost always, we do not have to eat as much as we do. A psychological component to eating enters the picture, and then eating becomes salvation. Some foods are judged as bad or sinful, and others as good or spiritual, or they just make us feel happy. The issue is not to *not* eat what we like and enjoy, but to eat without making a big deal about it. As bodies we all have preferences, and therefore we may as well eat and do what we enjoy eating and doing, and not eat and not do what we do not like, as long as we are not behaving in ways that are hurtful to ourselves or others. The fact of the matter is that eating will not awaken us from the dream, nor will breathing or any form of special/dependent relationship. No addiction can awaken us from the dream.

(W-pI.76.1:2-4) Each [of these "senseless things": special relationships] **has imprisoned you with laws as senseless as itself. You are not bound by them. Yet to understand that this is so, you must first realize salvation lies not there.**

As long as our body is seen as a classroom, we need to keep it healthy, physically and psychologically, which means we need to do whatever makes our body function well, physically and psychologically. If we do this with the Holy Spirit, our behavior will not be harmful. But done with the ego, our behavior will always be harmful because our purpose will be to separate and therefore attack. We know we are listening to the ego when we make a big deal about the body's needs or activities, just as we know we are listening to the Holy Spirit when we place emphasis only on the decision-making mind's choice for the ego or Holy Spirit. Only that decision matters.

(W-pI.76.1:5) While you would seek for it [for salvation] **in things that have no meaning, you bind yourself to laws that make no sense.**

What has no meaning includes anything that has to do with form. Within the world of perception, where $2 + 2 = 4$, nothing can bring us salvation. As already discussed, *A Course in Miracles* will never bring us salvation. It is merely a book, part of the world of form. *Living* what this course says is another story, however. Believing that a person named Jesus will help or save us is a special relationship. But seeing him as a symbol of our right-minded decision—that we are asking for help to choose our right mind— *will* save us because we would not be seeing Jesus as different from us. His eyes may be more open than ours, but we are still the same. This course cannot give us a wisdom that is not already in us. Each of us has the same Holy Spirit, the same voice Helen "listened" to. Its wisdom is in everyone.

As with true education, *A Course in Miracles* simply awakens us to what is already within. I have

mentioned other times that Plato defined education as
"reminiscence" (*anamnesis*): people remember what
already is in them. A teacher does not give students
something they do not have, but reminds them of
what they already know. The truth is in everyone;
otherwise it can be in no one. Jesus does not have
a special corner on the truth. He just knows there is
nothing but that truth. We, on the other hand, have
replaced truth with our special love objects.

Again, "While you seek for salvation in things that
have no meaning, you bind yourself to laws that make
no sense." These are the world's laws of $2 + 2 = 4$,
the "real" world in which things happen because of
natural laws. On the contrary, things happen here
because we made the world to have things happen.
Everything that happens in this world bespeaks
separation. That is the reason we should trust nothing
in this world, and in the end, should trust no one who
teaches us about the world, unless that person knows
that $2 + 2 = 5$.

By way of clarification, these guidelines about
whom to trust apply even to one's choice of a heart
surgeon or financial advisor, for example, as long as
that person knows that $2 + 2$ is also 4! Personally,
I would always prefer to do business with someone
who knows both, but that does not always happen. I

hope it is clear that even though $2 + 2 = 5$, in order to be in this world and learn from it, you have to know that $2 + 2 = 4$ as well. If you are going to be a surgeon, you had better know how the body works and have skillful hands that can operate. I think it helps to have surgeons who know $2 + 2 = 5$, but I would not make my choice based on that alone. That is why I have always urged Course students who need a therapist not to go to a so-called *Course in Miracles* therapist, because Course therapists—though not all of them— tend to focus too heavily on $2 + 2 = 5$; i.e, the world is an illusion. What they are really doing is skipping over $2 + 2 = 4$ because they are so guilty about it, often leading to disastrous results for the patient who may already be suffering from denial. Ideally you want someone who has mastered the world's arithmetic, but who also knows that its arithmetic is an illusion.

Again, salvation is found in one place and one place only: the decision-making part of our mind that chose the ego and damnation, and can now reverse itself and choose salvation. Jesus cannot save us; the Holy Spirit cannot save us; *A Course in Miracles* cannot save us. They can only remind us that *we* are the savior. The only power in the entire universe that can save us is the power of our mind to choose. That is God's law as expressed in this world. If God's law is God's Will, and His law is perfect Oneness and Love, its reflection in this world is our choosing the thought system of forgiveness that reflects His Will.

It follows, then, that in this world "I am under no laws but God's" pertains to the law of decision. I can choose to see someone as separate from me or the same as I am. I can choose to live my life following the ego's principle of separate interests or Jesus' principle of shared interests. I am the only one who can do that. All this course does is remind us that we have a mind, and that this mind is all-powerful with the ability to choose Heaven or earth.

The final sentence in the paragraph:

(W-pI.76.1:6) Thus do you seek to prove salvation is where it is not.

We seek to prove salvation is in the world and in the laws the world makes. Thus, the law of $2 + 2 = 4$, if looked at from the perspective of Christianity, is that you read the Bible, believe the Bible, and take Jesus Christ as your Lord and Savior. But that reeks with specialness, for it is all about making the world real and making the words of the Bible different from all other words. If there is *no hierarchy of illusions*, then the Bible can be no different from any other book. *A Course in Miracles* is no different from any other book. All that is important is the Voice reflected in the blue book. The Voice, not the form, is the only meaningful factor. The aforementioned laws of relationships, medicine, health, and money that Jesus talks about in paragraph 8 also include the "laws" of religion:

> Perhaps you even think that there are laws which set forth what is God's and what is yours. Many "religions" have been based on this. [Note the quotation marks around "religions."] They would not save but damn in Heaven's name (W-pI.76.8:4-6).

Why would religions damn? Because they separate. They say this is what is God's and this is what is yours. Yours is the world of sin, and God's is the world of perfect Love. They are both real, as are sin and sinlessness, and God sees both. Once we believe the lie and put it in the mouth of God Himself, building religions upon it, we are justified in dividing the world into the sinful and sinless, the good and bad, the true believers and pagans/heretics/ infidels. Now there is a law, a divine law, which is but another hateful form of the ego's law of $2 + 2 = 4$.

People do the same thing with this course. Once again, *Nothing so blinding as perception of form.*

Form lies. Earlier in the text Jesus says that special relationships express the triumph of form over content, the ego over God (T-16.V:10:1; 12:2)—the essence of all formal religions. Form always lies because it separates and divides, making the world real. Please do not do that with *A Course in Miracles*. Do not use it as a way to separate yourself from Jesus, from other students of the Course, or from those who are not students. If God's Son is one, this course is meant for only one person: *you*. When your mind is healed, you know the oneness is not you, but *all* God's Sons.

(W-pI.76.2:1-2) Today we will be glad you cannot prove it [i.e., prove that salvation is where it is not: in the laws of the world or body]. **For if you could, you would forever seek salvation where it is not, and never find it.**

That is why formal religions never work. They are always based on form, which is why they are called "formal." They have a set of laws and rituals, holy books, people, places, objects—all of which separate. Since the world is an illusion, there cannot be anything here that is holy or unholy. If God's Son is one, there cannot be holy *and* unholy people. If God's Word is soundless, abstract, and non-specific,

It cannot be contained in a book or limited by words. The workbook, in fact, tells us that God does not understand our "little prayers" (W-pI.183.7:3), and from the manual: "God does not understand words, for they were made by separated minds to keep them in the illusion of separation" (M-21.1:7). And so we cannot reach God with words. Nothing here has any reality. Nothing! Remember, the world lies, and the laws of this world are all designed to keep us rooted in the illusion. As long as we are rooted here, we are rooted in the thought system that made the world, without even knowing there is such a thought system. This demonstrates just how fiendishly clever the ego is.

(W-pI.76.2:3-5) The idea for today tells you once again how simple is salvation. Look for it where it waits for you, and there it will be found. Look nowhere else, for it is nowhere else.

Where is salvation? In the mind. Where is it not? In the world, in the body, in anything specific. Anything specific is $2 + 2 = 4$. It is not of God and therefore is not true. Since we made specifics to attack and to keep us separate, we have to use the same specifics to lead us back to the thought of attack so we can correct it. That is how a special relationship becomes holy. When Jesus tells us that the Holy Spirit does not take our special relationships away but transforms them, he means that the Holy Spirit transforms the relationship's *purpose* (see, for example, T-15.V.5; T-18.II.6; T-25.VI.4). He does not do anything with the form, with bodies. Not only is He not interested in bodies, He does not see them—there aren't any! Bodies are hallucinatory. Do you want the Holy Spirit or Jesus to be psychotic, to see what is not there? Do not ask Their help with your body or another person's. Rather, ask for help to shift your attention from the body to the mind, of which the body is the projection. Our Teachers are in the mind, the locus of salvation. That is where the problem and its answer are. Look for salvation where it waits for you, in the mind, and do not look for it anywhere else.

In a sense, these two very simple sentences: "Look for it where it waits for you, and there it will be found. Look nowhere else, for it is nowhere else," sum up the entire Course, which is about returning our attention to the mind. The world's laws and customs—what is appropriate and not appropriate, right and not right, holy and not holy, loving and not loving—are all based on the law of 2 + 2 equaling 4, the strategy of keeping us mindless. This is how the ego controls us, keeping us mindless so we never get back to where the problem is: the decision-making mind. People cannot control us. Nothing in this world can control us. *We* control us. This is extremely important to understand; otherwise we will continue to get caught in the ego's trap of duality. The "mind control" that people talk about is really brain control. Of course brains can be controlled, *but there is no brain*. So it is merely nothing that is being controlled by nothing. This is not evil or sinful. It is silly, deserving only the Holy Spirit's gentle laughter. No one can control your mind because it is not part of the body, nor is it in it. The body is in the mind because ideas *leave not their source*, not the other way around. That is why we are under no laws but God's.

We need recall that there is nothing out here that can affect us. This does not mean we should deny that the mind is still focused on the body and that we want to be mindless, at which point we have placed ourselves under the world's laws. This is the case, even though we consciously protest that we are helplessly trapped in a body we did not make. Not only does perception lie, but so does our experience. The truth remains that while the world can affect our bodies and brains, it can do nothing to the decision-making mind. This is the good news the Course brings us.

Jesus cannot do anything to the mind. He is simply a presence of love, light, and sanity in the separated mind. His very presence is the light that calls us back to the problem (having chosen the wrong teacher) and says, "Choose me." Once again, there are undoubtedly people and events that have power over the body—the body, after all, does have power over the body—but these are worldly laws. What do they have to do with us if we are a mind? This is the meaning of the lesson, another attempt to help us break the mold so we can see that 2 + 2 is not 4, but 5. This frees us to see that nothing in the world has power to take God's Love and peace from our minds.

Had there been no religious language in this lesson, Dostoevsky's underground man would have loved it because it is really about 2 + 2 being 5, not 4, the reason we are not bound by anything here. However, as long as we see images of ourselves every morning in the bathroom mirror and recognize them—whether we are pleased by the images or not—we know we are under the body's laws. It is never helpful to deny that, though we must not believe that the laws have any real power. They have power *only* because the mind has given them the power. If people affect us, it is because our minds have given them the power to affect us. And therein lies our freedom. The underground man's goal was to be free, which was impossible if 2 + 2 was always 4. He wanted the freedom to say that 2 + 2 sometimes is 5. Lesson 76 gives us all that freedom because freedom lies in the mind's power to choose between the Holy Spirit's truth and the ego's illusion, between forgiveness as the reigning principle of our lives and attack. This is true power, and it is something within our control once we remember we are minds.

(W-pI.76.3:1) Think of the freedom in the recognition that you are not bound by all the strange and twisted laws you have set up to save you.

In the text Jesus teaches that the way out of suffering is to "look upon the problem as it is, and not the way that you have set it up" (T-27.VII.2:2). That is freedom. The way we have set it up is that we are bound because 2 + 2 = 4 and we cannot change that. One of the more powerful laws of this world is attack. We got here because we attacked God and then believed that God was going to attack us in return. Running away, we made up a world in which everyone attacks everyone else because that is the world's origin and nature. It was made as an attack on God because it came from the thought of separation that was an attack on God. How, then, could attack not be the rule here, a rule that binds us? There is no way out of this except through the principle of *kill or be killed*. This is the heart of every special relationship: I will steal from (kill) you before you steal from (kill) me.

Freedom lies in realizing we can transcend the ego's laws, but not by denying the body, starving or indulging it. We transcend the body by looking honestly at it, as it is, not as we have set it up. We made the body for the purpose of saying that 2 + 2 = 4 so we do not have to look at what we think is much worse, that 1 + 1 = 2. The insane mind is the source of our guilt and terror. We set the world and body up in such a way that we would not realize it is a farce, made up to have us believe that 2 + 2 = 4, and 1 + 1 = 2. Recognizing this set-up is what frees us.

If you are sick, by all means take care of your body and use whatever magic works to help your body feel better, psychologically or physically. But somewhere inside realize that 2 + 2 = 5. Your pain does not come from whatever you think it comes from, nor does its undoing come from whatever you think has curative power. What is played out externally are decisions the mind has made: decisions for the ego or decisions to turn away from the ego.

To say "I am under no laws but God's" is to look at the reflection of God's laws in the world. Love is reflected in our seeing everyone as the same. The law of God's Will is reflected in our making the choice to say that $2 + 2 = 5$: the world is not what we thought, and pain and guilt come not from anything external, but from the mind's decision. Now that we know this, we can truly ask Jesus to help us return to the mind and choose again. If we do not choose again, at least we know why: we are still afraid of love, still afraid of letting go of specialness, still afraid of awakening from the dream. At least now we know what the problem is, seeing it as it is and not how we have set it up. This recognition is all our teacher asks of us, and why he speaks of a "little willingness" (T-18.IV). We do not have to change anything, nor make ourselves believe that $2 + 2 = 5$. We merely have to know we are choosing to believe in the laws of the world—$2 + 2 = 4$—because we are afraid that $2 + 2 = 5$, and that would mean all our defenses have not worked. We do not fear the ego; we fear its nothingness. At least now we know what we are doing, and can honor and respect the decision to be afraid without blaming anyone else.

Now comes our famous line:

(W-pI.76.3:2-4) You really think that you would starve unless you have stacks of green paper strips and piles of metal discs. You really think a small round pellet or some fluid pushed into your veins through a sharpened needle will ward off disease and death. You really think you are alone unless another body is with you.

Jesus is poking fun at the silliness of believing all this. Yet we all do. He is not saying *not* to earn money, eat, go to a doctor, have sex, or be in relationships. He is simply saying that as we behave as normal bodies, we should realize the body is not what we think it is. Satisfying the body will not awaken us from the dream, but what will awaken us is satisfying the body and knowing it is not the body we are satisfying. We are really satisfying the ego's need to keep us bodies instead of minds. This is all we need to know. *2 + 2 = 5, not 4.*

We made the body in such a way that when it has feelings, they are so strong they cannot be denied. If you have not eaten or taken a drink of water in a long time, you will feel the lack. We all know how strong rage and sexual feelings are. Yet even though they can feel overpowering at times, they are not what they seem. Feelings do not emanate from the body but from the mind. For example, a puppet does not feel angry, sexual, or have an anxiety attack. It is only the mind's decision to use the body as a distraction that leads to these feelings. Therefore, how could they be bad or wonderfully pleasurable? This is why the Course urges us not to deny our experiences, but to look past them to see the purpose of our learning that we are minds and not bodies. Jesus never tells us not to get angry, but merely not to justify our anger (e.g., T-30.VI.1:1). He is teaching us to use our bodily experiences to serve a different purpose: the mind's forgiveness instead of the body's attack. Bodies lie, for they were made to conceal the mind as the cause of all feelings. And so feelings are not what they seem; 2 + 2 does not equal 4.

All this lesson is asking is for us to look at what is going on. That's all. Again, Jesus is not telling us not to have relationships, sex, earn money, eat, or go to doctors. This is the misunderstanding that has caused and continues to cause so many problems with students since the Course's publication in 1976. He is simply saying that at the same time we are adding up 2 and 2 and getting 4, we want to learn that the real answer is 5. We will not know it is 5, though, until we first learn the world's answer of 4. And so we are not to deny the body or the satisfaction of its different needs, only to remember that they are not what they seem. Anything the body does or feels is a result of the mind's decision made for the ego or the Holy Spirit. Nothing else is necessary to understand, which is why it bears frequent repeating.

If the body is used to keep you separate from others, know that you chose your ego. If the body and its feelings are used to have you realize that you and another person are not separate (you have the same split mind), then you know you chose the Holy Spirit. If what you do on the level of form (the body) does not exclude other people on the level of content (the mind), then you know Jesus is your teacher. Bodies have to exclude. You cannot have lunch with everyone. You cannot have sex with everyone. You cannot be with everyone. But even though you are with one person or a few people, that does not have to exclude anyone else in content or thought. This is not about behavior. There is no good or bad behavior; there are no appropriate or inappropriate feelings. All behavior and feelings are neutral. What alone is meaningful is which teacher you ask to help you with them. The purpose determines whether what you are doing is of the right or wrong mind, not the activity of itself. Anything of the body will exclude (special love and hate) because that is why bodies were made.

But the *meaning* of behavior depends on the mind's purpose.

So again, when we read paragraph 3, especially sentences 2 through 4, we need understand that Jesus is not saying that we should not live normal lives. He is saying that as we partake in normal bodily activities, we should have him with us. Then whatever we do, whomever we are involved with, will be holy because we have taken the thought of holiness with us. In time we will realize that the thought of holiness is not Jesus; it is everyone, including us and him. Holiness, coming from God, cannot be separating or differentiating, nor is it specific.

On Level One, everything of the body is illusory and only things of God are true. On Level Two, everything here is illusory, but what is important is with whom you behave: the ego or Jesus. As Hamlet said, there is nothing good or bad, but thinking makes it so. There is nothing right or wrong, except for the person you choose as your teacher. If it is the ego it is wrong. If it is Jesus it is right. Yet this does not refer to behavior or form. Remember, do not listen to anyone who thinks 2 + 2 is only 4. But you most definitely listen to our elder brother because he knows 2 + 2 = 5, at the same time he urges you to learn that 2 + 2 = 4. Avoiding this worldly learning is a defense against knowing that $2 + 2 = 5$, for it is the essential stepping-stone toward it.

(W-pI.76.4:1) It is insanity that thinks these things.

This is a gentle way of telling us we are insane, because the fact is that everyone who believes the world to be real thinks this way. Again, anyone who thinks that $2 + 2 = 4$ is insane. Jesus says in the text that we are always asking "the only thing in all the universe that does not know" to tell us what reality is—we are always asking the body, or the ego, to tell us what is true (T-20.III.7:5-7). That is why we all think $2 + 2 = 4$. That is why we believe we have to eat and breathe, need money to survive, need people to combat loneliness, and why, when we get sick, we need medicine and other things to help us. All this reflects our intrinsic insanity.

The idea here is not to deny the insanity or indulge in reaction formation by pretending the opposite: I do not have to go to the doctor because my mind is so holy, etc.—as if *not* going to the doctor makes you holy. What matters is that you go to the Doctor in your mind. *That* matters. At that point you go to the earthly doctor or you don't, but you realize that salvation does not depend on going or not going. If you think it does, then the ego has caught you once more. To quote Hamlet again: "The lady doth protest too much, methinks." Everyone here protests too much. When you dramatically profess your love for someone, whether to a person, Jesus, God, or even this course, you know that is a defense against the opposite. Truth and love are quiet, and need not make assertions. It need not speak in a loud voice. The Holy Spirit is described as a "still, small voice," a phrase from the Old Testament (1 Kings). Dostoevsky's underground man rants and raves; Jesus does not. It matters not if you go or do not go to a doctor, have sex or be celibate, be rich or poor. *It matters only with whom you do these things*.

Thus, at the same time you are doing what every normal body does, there is a part of you that knows that $2 + 2 = 5$, which means what seems to be happening here is really occurring in the mind. You therefore will appear normal, but really are not because in this world normal people say $2 + 2 = 4$, believing that there are external (read: bodily) causes for what they do and say. This passes for normality here. But when people really learn that $2 + 2 = 5$, they are no longer normal, even though they look as if they are. They do not advertise their "abnormality." They simply are, looking like everyone else but, once more, smiling more frequently, with foreheads that are serene and eyes that are quiet (W-pI.155.1:2-3). There is a peace about them, and a love that is not special, for it embraces everyone. Love cannot do that in form, but its content excludes no one.

(W-pI.76.4:1-4) It is insanity that thinks these things. You call them laws, and put them under different names in a long catalogue of rituals that have no use and serve no purpose. You think you must obey the "laws" [note the quotes] **of medicine, of economics and of health. Protect the body, and you will be saved.**

Importantly again, Jesus is not saying not to protect the body. He is certainly not saying we should deny it, as we have seen. The challenge is that while on the one hand we do not deny the body, on the other hand we do not believe in its reality. Jesus is not saying not to obey the laws of medicine, economics, and health, since we still believe we are bodies, but rather that we want to learn from him that there is another way of looking at the body. While learning that $2 + 2 = 4$, we are also being taught that it is 5 and that the world lies.

We all know people who try to take perfect care of their bodies. There is nothing wrong with that, but the problem arises when the underlying thought is: "I am going to make my body perfect because I feel so imperfect." That thought, then, can never change because it has been covered over by having a healthy, youthful body. Beautiful bodies, however, do not make for beautiful minds, which can occur only when you have chosen the teacher of beauty. Love is the mind's beauty, but if you feel you are "the home of evil, darkness and sin" (W-pI.93.1:1), the ego will lead you to the reaction formation of denying your perceived ugliness by making a beautiful home, family, and car. Above all, you will strive to have a beautiful body—youthful, energetic, healthy, and attractive. There is nothing sinful about taking care of your body, but if you have an investment in having your body look a certain way, then you know you are defending against the opposite feeling in your mind. Reaction formation is one of the basic laws of the split mind. Recall: we react against what we believe inside by doing the opposite outside.

To make this very clear, this does not mean you should not groom yourself, take care of yourself, and do whatever makes your body feel good and look attractive. Just be certain about what you are doing and realize that this will not heal your mind. If the purpose of your studying *A Course in Miracles* is to heal your mind so you can awaken from this dream and go home, then denying that something in your mind has to be healed will not further that aim. There is nothing wrong in doing anything with your body as long as it is used as a way to heal your mind. Thus, at the same time you are making your body attractive, keep in mind that you are insane in thinking this will make your mind attractive. It has nothing to do with your mind, which of course is the whole purpose of being invested in how your body looks.

To repeat, we need only look openly at what we do. The way we have set it up is we think that if people find our bodies attractive—brains, strength, bank account, etc.—that makes us a good person and people will worship at our altar. "All that is needed is you look upon the problem as it is, and not the way that you have set it up" (T-27.VII.2:2). That is all Jesus says is required of us. He comments on that sentence, but he does not add anything. We do not have to change our behavior. He is not saying *not* to shower or wear nice clothes. He is saying only that we need to watch our thoughts as we groom ourselves every morning: this will appeal to this person, or to a person I haven't met yet. Everyone does this, and it is hardly sinful. It just will not get us home. What will get us home is looking at what we are doing without judgment and without taking our egos so seriously.

Elsewhere, Jesus uses the expression "bait to catch another fish" (T-24.VII.4:6) to describe our use of the body. We need to acknowledge that this is what we are doing, saying: "I will really feel better when I get another victim to fall into my trap. I really believe it will make me feel good to have people look at my body and be attracted to it." It may make our body feel better, and it will certainly make our ego feel better, but it will not awaken us from the dream. And if we are serious about wanting to awaken, we will not necessarily stop what we are doing, but we will look with Jesus at what we are doing. He will not tell us to stop putting on makeup, shaving, or picking out clothes to wear. He will simply ask us to look at what we are doing and think about its purpose: Do you really think this will bring you closer to him and his love, or closer to God? Simply ask yourself the question.

Near the beginning of Chapter 24 Jesus tells us: "To learn this course requires willingness to question every value that you hold" (T-24.in.2:1). He does not say that we need to let the value go, or that we should take his value instead of ours. He merely says, "question every value"; question the value of making yourself beautiful, sexually alluring, or intellectually appealing. Just watch yourself. That's all. At some point, if you do this with Jesus you will realize the silliness of what you do. This does not mean you will not dress nicely or look attractive, but it does mean that you won't take yourself quite as seriously as you used to, having an investment in looking a certain way. We don't break the ego's laws; we simply look at their purpose. When we make extensive preparations to present our bodies, we follow the laws of specialness: people will like me if I act, dress, or make up my face a certain way, and will not if I don't. Conscious of them or not, we all follow these laws.

Laws operate in this world, but people have different laws and different ways of interpreting them. They are all insane, for they are all about separating. We cannot see the Christ in others when we see them as fish we are luring with the bait of our bodies. Once again, this specialness does not make us evil or sinful. But after a while it does make us look silly, at least to ourselves. At some point we must ask what all this has to do with the mind. And the answer, of course, is: Nothing! And this is exactly why we do it—because it has nothing to do with the mind. We are terrified of the mind and think we are terrified of the thought that $1 + 1 = 2$, because that arouses the guilt over the separation along with the fear of God's retaliative wrath. Yet what we really fear is that $1 + 1 = 1$, has always equaled 1, and will forever equal 1, no matter what we think we have done. This, the only true equation, marks the end of our specialness. In order to protect this separated and dualistic self, we use the body and all its laws to keep ourselves mindless—rooted in a world where $2 + 2 = 4$. This prevents us from returning to the mind where $1 + 1 = 2$, and beyond that to the remembrance that $1 + 1 = 1$.

To recap briefly, the insanity of our experience of living in the world is that the body is treated as something real. That is the basic mistake. The clear strategy of the ego in making up the world was to render us mindless. There is always a method in the ego's madness. If we forget we have a mind and relate only to the body, believing that the body is caused by other bodies or physical events outside it such as genes and relationships, then the mind is kept totally secret. If the mind is secret and we do not know we have one, we can never change it, and if we can never change our minds, the original decision for the ego remains intact.

As I mentioned earlier, purpose is one of the most important themes in *A Course in Miracles*. Purpose is everything. If you understand the purpose, you understand the meaning of any situation, relationship, sickness, or anything else. The purpose of the world, once again, is to keep us mindless. That is the name of the ego's game, the consummation of its strategy. The ego is the thought of attack on God, the thought that God's Love and Oneness can be compromised, if not obliterated. The world is the projection of that thought (see W-pII.3.2:1), but now we think the world is the problem because once we project the thought from the mind onto the body and the world, a veil of forgetfulness falls across our minds, resulting in our having no recollection of where we came from.

On the macrocosmic level the ego made the world and the entire physical universe, and on the microcosmic level it made the body. However, we have no awareness that our minds did this, nor that the world has never left its source in the mind. In other words, we simply think that we exist outside the mind. This is similar to our experience of watching a movie. Psychologically we think there are people on the screen. Our intellects understand the situation, but we react emotionally as if there were real people in front of us. We form relationships with the characters on the screen, but the fact of the matter is that what is there is a projection of a film running through a machine in back of us. There is only the illusion of reality. That is Jesus' point. There is no one here. When he says "There is no world!" (W-pI.132.6:2), he means that literally. There is a great deal in *A Course in Miracles* that is meant symbolically or metaphorically, but not that statement.

The protection of the body is exactly what the ego wants, which makes perfect sense within a world where the ego rules. The laws here do not really hold because they are totally made up. Their purpose is to keep us rooted here. Thus if we think an object falls because of the law of gravity, we think there is a law of gravity. Well, what I am holding in my hand falls because we all have a collective dream in which we made up a law of gravity, so that when we drop an object, it falls. There is no law of gravity, just as there is no object. Again, "Protect the body, and you will be saved." That is how we all live, and so Jesus tells us again:

(W-pI.76.5:1) These are not laws, but madness.

Whenever we get upset and come to Jesus, he helps us by telling us that what we are upset about is not there. We will experience his loving help in whatever form we can accept, but the content is always the same: $2 + 2 = 5$, not 4; there is nothing outside the mind that can hurt us. We will get that message in whatever form we can accept without fear, which is why it is important not to overemphasize the hearing of specific messages. Jesus' answer is non-specific, being love. Our minds then turn the love into something specific, and that is why we have to be so careful. The real answer we want is the answer that says $2 + 2 = 5$: "Do not let anything here have power over you. At any given moment you can choose my love instead of whatever is out there, and in that choice for my love you will be at peace." This is the message of the lesson. Jesus is not saying, "Come with me and I will teach you how to walk on water, or that you will never have to see a doctor again." He does not care if you see a doctor. He does not know about doctors because he does not know about bodies, which don't exist. I cannot emphasize that enough. When you become upset by what happens in the world, personally or collectively, you are falling into the ego's mindless trap. Everything that seems to occur here is in the mind: *ideas leave not their source.*

The clearest analogy is what happens when we dream at night. No matter what is going on in our dream, when we open our eyes we are still in bed. Similarly, when we open our eyes after accepting the Atonement, we are still in our mind. We have remained thought, and everything we think we see here dissolves—just as when a movie is over it fades out and the screen is blank. This will all be blank because there was never anything here. We react as if there were something here, but Jesus is telling us this is madness, sheer madness.

What is helpful on a practical level as we go through our day and begin to get upset about things is to realize the world is not what we think it is. One more time: "All that is needed is you look upon the problem as it is, and not the way you have set it up." We have set up our world so there would be a problem out there that needs attention. The ego, as we have seen, is fiendishly and maliciously clever. We know its strategy is brilliant because it has worked for eons. Look at all the different forms of religions and spiritualities. With very few exceptions they end up keeping us mindless, and making God mindless by giving Him the role of creating the world, and then having Him do things in the illusion. Despite the compelling nature of the physical world, it remains but an illusion.

(W-pI.76.5:2-3) The body is endangered by the mind that hurts itself. The body suffers just in order that the mind will fail to see it is a victim of itself.

"The body is endangered by the mind that hurts itself." A very clear, declarative sentence! We cannot complain about triple negatives or blank verse. The danger is never in the nonexistent world, but in the mind's decision to make guilt real, and then project it out making us mindless: vulnerable, helpless, and at the mercy of forces beyond our control. Thus we are not responsible for our disquiet, disease, depression, or despair, because the causes are our genes, hormones, parents, the world, evildoers, the president, the weather, the stock market, or whatever. *A Course in Miracles* teaches us simply that all this is madness.

The mind hurts itself when it chooses the ego as its teacher instead of Jesus. The lines we just read make perfect sense, but what makes putting them into practice so difficult is that when we go back into the world where its many voices are shouting at us (including our own), we experience it as being very real. As Wordsworth said, "The world is too much with us." It is a wonderful line and he was a great poet, but the world is not too much with us. The wrong mind is too much with us, but we like to think it is the world. Remember, the ego's strategy is only to keep us mindless. As long as we are mindless, the ego never has a thing to worry about. Remember, too, the ego is not the devil or a separated entity. The ego is the part of us that likes being us: individual, unique, special, and mindless.

One can well ask, if it is our dream and our world, why did we do such a terrible job of it? The fact of the matter is that we did *not* do a terrible job. Quite the opposite: we did brilliantly. Part of our perverse insanity is that we love it when things go wrong in the world. In fact, we made the world so that things would go wrong in it. As long as they do, with things breaking down and horrific events happening on all levels, as they always have and always will, our attention is riveted here. We then need to fix things, whether a disease on an individual level or the disease of mankind with its cruelty and viciousness, its suffering and pain. One cannot easily dismiss the absolutely ingenious nature of the dream; the evidence for the world's reality is so palpably real. Moreover, we never put the one witness on the stand that would disprove the ego's case: the body. The body lies and was made to lie, yet we ask it to tell us what reality is (T-20.III.7). We ask all the world's brilliant brain-bodies to tell us how things work here, why they do not work, and what we should do about it. And the body's true nature is never revealed because its lies are never exposed.

To repeat, don't go for help to those who believe $2 + 2 = 4$, because whatever they tell you, no matter how intelligent the answer, they will not lead you home. They may be helpful with your body, but they will not help you heal your mind. Don't all of us who study this course want our mind healed? Otherwise why would we bother with it? The problem is we are not aware of the other part of us that does not want our mind healed, and that is what we have to get in touch with, what Freud called *resistance*. If you are sincere and serious about wanting your mind healed, to awaken from the dream and return home, the only way you can do that is to realize the world lies. Everything here lies, including the body. Once again, $2 + 2 = 5$. There is no other way to return to the original equation—$1 + 1 = 1$—except by recognizing the difference between truth and illusion.

And so, we need to be in touch with how much we do not want to learn Jesus' arithmetic, how much we still want to be spiritually mindless, as well as want a Jesus who is spiritually mindless, not to mention a mindless God Himself. This is why people form religions, and why students take the Course, which is very clear about not being a religion, and try to turn it into one—with rituals, holy people, holy meetings, etc., reveling in the schisms and factions that are an inevitable part of the history of any religion or spirituality. This is *a* spiritual path, not anything else. Always keep in mind that the ego's goal is to keep us mindless, which means to root our attention in the differentiating and separating world of bodies and forms, at the expense of the mind's content.

(W-pI.76.5:4) The body's suffering is a mask the mind holds up to hide what really suffers.

This, too, is a very clear statement. What really suffers? Only the decision-making mind that chooses the ego. That alone suffers, because when we choose the ego we are choosing a belief in sin and guilt, and with that comes the terror that God is going to destroy us. There is no worse feeling than guilt (self-hatred). Even physical pain has an end, but the psychological pain of intense guilt that all of us carry is seemingly forever. Imagine the guilt of the horrific belief we destroyed Heaven: we took the pure Love of God, dragged it through the sewer, and out came specialness smelling like a rose, except it does not smell like a rose at all. This self-accusation is the source of all pain.

We take this pain in the mind and displace it onto the body, which now suffers. Bodies were made to suffer, individually and collectively. They suffer from disease, from the mad disease of the insane who believe they will feel better by destroying others. Everyone here is mentally ill, for everyone has the same mad belief, whether it is about dropping bombs or having an angry thought. There is certainly a difference between those two in this world, because people think $2 + 2 = 4$, but there is no real difference. Twice, Jesus says that a mild twinge of annoyance is a veil drawn across the face of intense fury (W-pI.21.2:3-5; M-17.4:4-7). There is no difference between an angry, judgmental thought and building a bomb and dropping it. They both are hateful, and both are attempts to define the problem as we set it up (in the world) rather than as it is (in the mind). The body's suffering was made to conceal the suffering that is in the guilt-laden mind, for once we are mindless we do not know about guilt. We know only that our bodies or the bodies of our loved ones hurt.

(W-pI.76.5:5) It would not understand it is its own enemy; that it attacks itself and wants to die.

The mind does not understand it is its own enemy—"it attacks itself and wants to die"—and projects its thought system of guilt and punishment onto the body. This means that the mind is the enemy, not cancer, disease, war, or even God. More precisely, the decision maker choosing the ego is the enemy, just as the decision maker choosing the Holy Spirit is salvation. Our happiness and disquiet come from the same place: the mind's decision.

(W-pI.76.5:6-7) It is from this your "laws" would save the body. It is for this you think you are a body.

The ego tells us we will be saved if we are bodies, if we listen to the world's voices tell us what is right and wrong, healthy and not healthy, spiritual and not spiritual. But the world is insane. The truth is that if we stay with the content and not the form, we will always be safe, because the danger is the ego's content of guilt, and the protection is the Holy Spirit's content of love. We need to stay with the content, for the problem and solution are both in the decision-making mind.

This will help us understand why *A Course in Miracles* is so difficult. It is not just another self-help system, another teaching that says we should forgive instead of judge, trust the Love of God instead of fearing it, and that we should take Jesus' hand to lead us home. This is a spirituality that teaches the difference between the mindless and mindful, and how everything here is mindless. Recognizing this will help us know what this course is truly saying, as well as understand who Jesus is and how he can help us. Our elder brother is a symbol, which means he does not exist. We are a symbol, which means we do not exist. But because we symbolize separation and Jesus symbolizes Atonement, we need his symbol to help us awaken from the dreams of separation, guilt, and specialness. We are speaking of the mind, the level of thought, which is why it makes no sense to compare the Jesus of the Bible with the Jesus of *A Course in Miracles*. It would be like comparing apples and oranges, mindlessness and mindfulness. The Jesus of the gospels is all about the mindless body—its sin and salvation—while the Jesus in *A Course in Miracles* is only about the mind and not the body at all. He says, for example, in direct refutation of the Catholic theology of the Eucharist: "Yet would I offer you my body, you whom I love, *knowing* its littleness?" (T-19.IV-A.17:5), meaning its nothingness. Instead, he is offering us his healed mind, which is our healed mind as well.

(W-pI.76.6:1-2) There are no laws except the laws of God. This needs repeating, over and over, until you realize it applies to everything that you have made in opposition to God's Will.

8. "I Am Under No Laws but God's"

When Jesus says "everything" he means *everything*, because the world was made in opposition to God's Will of perfect Oneness. Everything here is perfect separation, and Jesus is telling us this applies to everything we have made. In other words, we are not to take anything here seriously, which means not giving anything here power to take away our mind's experience of peace and love. This certainly does not mean laughing at people's suffering, to ignore or become insensitive to pain. It means not to give the world power to destroy God's Love and the love of His Son. We need to practice this, which we do by paying attention when we are upset, impatient, enraged, or excited about something. We need to become aware that the world is not as it seems, as our friend Plato taught over twenty-five hundred years ago.

The only way to practice this lesson, "I am under no laws but God's," and not become thoroughly confused is to realize it is true only if we are minds. As bodies we are clearly under the world's laws, and once we decide to be born we identify with them. Developmental laws govern our passage from infancy into childhood, adolescence, and adulthood, and finally old age and death. While there are variations and individual differences within these laws, no one escapes them because we all die. For example, it is a law that eyes change with age. But this does not happen universally, although death does. Bodies do change and do eventually die, not because of the body's laws—there are no such laws—but because our minds chose to become bodies and to be subsumed under the mind's insane laws of separation, guilt, and punishment.

It takes vigilance and diligence to reverse one's thinking. It is very hard, for example, to read *A Course in Miracles* and not read it as a body. You can really see progress with this course when you recognize that Jesus is not addressing you as a person, but as the decision maker in the mind that is outside time and space. You know there has been a qualitative shift in your understanding of this material when you get past an intellectual understanding and truly experience that Jesus is not talking to a body. He is telling you there is no *you*, "There is no life outside of Heaven" (T-23.II.19:1). In "The Laws of Chaos" Jesus asks: "Can you paint rosy lips upon a skeleton, dress it in loveliness, pet it and pamper it, and make it live?" (T-23.II.18:8). Just because we dress the body up we think it is living. It is not living, so why would Jesus be talking to something that is not alive? He is addressing only the mind's decision maker.

Once again, *A Course in Miracles* is difficult, as is reversing our bodily identification, because we inevitably read it as a body. We are bodies, so we think, but one fine day it will dawn on us that we have been reading the Course wrongly. We will recognize that we need to go back to the beginning and read it again. We have been reading it as if we were bodies, thinking Jesus is a body talking to us as bodies about what we should and should not do with other bodies. Sure, we will admit, he talks about mind and says the body is not real, but he does not really mean it. We take that information, put it aside (dissociation), and blithely continue doing our spiritual work, thinking we are bodies and that we will return home as a body, as a person.

From this gross misperception of who we are, it is an obvious and natural question to ask: "What happens when we die?" But if we are not bodies, we do not die; if the body is not alive, how can it die? Nothing happens when we die because nothing happens when we think we live. That question can occur only to those who think they are bodies. This dynamic of repression, dissociation, and projection demonstrates the clever tricks the ego plays on us. We read this course that so clearly teaches—right from the beginning—that its only focus is the mind, and we ignore it and think Jesus is a person (body) talking to a person (body).

One more time, Jesus, or the symbol of love that his course represents, is communicating only to the decision maker in all of us. Moreover, since Jesus does not speak or have use for words, we are in truth communicating only to ourselves. Our minds choose love instead of fear, and Jesus and the Holy Spirit represent this love, although the world has many other symbols (C-5.1). Because we think we are bodies, our minds translate the non-specificity of love into a form we can relate to without fear. Consequently, we think Jesus is speaking to us as individual bodies. To reinforce this important thought, I want to briefly digress to talk about Helen.

On rare occasions Helen experienced the presence of non-ego love. I would be with her, and suddenly she would not be there. Her face would change, and when she spoke it was still Helen, but in a totally non-ego voice. It had no inflection, and was as if from another dimension. When she "returned" and her face regained its natural color, she described the experience as being beyond Jesus, beyond words. What she meant was that Jesus is specific, and this went beyond the symbol of Jesus to the pure Love of God that he represented. This was why when she spoke—I do not recall her words—it sounded other-worldly. It went beyond the specific, beyond words, beyond what she experienced as the person Jesus. At that point she was not the Helen I knew. It felt as if I were in a totally non-ego presence.

Very often I was with Helen when she was hearing messages from Jesus or writing them down. However holy the experience or beautiful the message, they remained dualistic. But the real "Helen" was beyond this when she was in that other-worldly state. Yet this is a state you cannot long remain in. In "Can God Be Reached Directly?" (M-26), the answer to the question is no, or if so, only for a very brief period of time. The reason is that you would not be able to stay here if the non-corporeal experience went on indefinitely. In those atemporal instants with Helen the face was hers, but it was transfigured or transformed. All I can say is that there was no ego in it. It was as if her worldly life had been drained, although she was very much alive. In Freud's terms, we would say there was no libido there, no energy. It happened maybe three, four, or five times in all the years I knew Helen, and when she came back from the experience she said it was beyond Jesus. This meant, again, that it was beyond anything specific. It was like being in the presence of pure love, a love that was not of this world. In that state there is no decision maker, for it is literally beyond the split mind.

In my book on Helen I called this the priestess side of Helen.* This "Helen" is the true source of *A Course in Miracles*. It is this non-ego presence in the Course that makes it so authoritative and impels people to respond to it as they do. In this very real sense, *A Course in Miracles* is beyond the specific symbol we call Jesus. It came through a person named Helen, whose mind translated into form—words and concepts—its non-specific and non-ego love. We would not be reading this book now if she had remained in that state. It was as if on a deeper level her mind chose to be Helen, with all the contradictory elements that comprised her personality and kept her here. She could not have taken this course down if she had identified as an egoless priestess.

I suspect that when Jesus was here, whoever we think he was, he was like that almost all the time. There was an other-worldly radiance and presence around him that would have made it difficult for people to stay in his presence and retain their egos. This is the reason people had to whittle him down to size and write stories as if he were a body and a person. If

---

* *Absence from Felicity: Helen Schucman and Her Scribing of A COURSE IN MIRACLES.* See Chapter 17 and the Epilogue.

you know anything about comparative mythologies, you will find many of these myths reflected in the New Testament tales. The writers superimposed these buried archetypal elements—their egos—onto this person, giving him a name and lineage, along with the events of this hero's miraculous life.

Again, *A Course in Miracles* came from that pure, non-ego love, but as long as Helen identified as Helen, the scribing became a dualistic experience in which the man Jesus talked to her and she wrote down what she heard. Most students know the story of her scribing, and the Helen stories I have told are true in the same way that $2 + 2 = 4$ is true. This means they are *not* true. Lovely stories to be sure, which symbolically express the truth to us who still think we are bodies. But the story is really about love, and love is not of this world or of bodies, though it can seem to take bodily form. This explains people's not really understanding Helen or the scribing of the Course, or the Course itself for that matter, *which is not about bodies*. Rather, *A Course in Miracles* is about going to the place of love that is in everyone's right mind. Helen did it, a wonderful example for all of us. Helen would always tell people that they could do what she did. Hearing *the* Voice is no big deal, because we all have that place of love to which we can go. However, once we think of Jesus as a person who lived two-thousand years ago, and think of ourselves as persons, we are in the world of myth and symbols, a world governed by laws where $2 + 2 = 4$.

And so, despite the moving nature of the Helen stories, if we take them as literally true, we are in trouble because $2 + 2$ is not 4. *A Course in Miracles* is really not a book, Jesus is not a body, nor is his course teaching bodies. It teaches our *minds* to choose against the thought of fear and for the thought of love. Truly understanding this will make us totally loving to everyone, because if Jesus and Helen are thoughts of love, so are we, as is this course. If, again, "there is no life outside of Heaven," the Course has as much life (or non-life) as we do. We—inanimate and animate forms alike—are merely symbols. We are symbols that look like bodies, and the Course is a symbol that looks like three books. Yet love stays the same, regardless of its forms. But wanting to preserve our individual identities, we strive to make the body special, just as we want to make Jesus, Helen, and this blue book special.

Reiterating the main point, this lesson will make no sense if we read it as a body, but will make perfect sense if we remember that Jesus is talking from a mind to a mind about a mind. We continue with the next sentence:

(W-pI.76.6:3) Your magic has no meaning.

In *A Course in Miracles*, *magic* is anything that is done externally to solve a problem that does not exist. The miracle is what is done internally to solve a problem that also does not exist. The difference is that magic solves the problem of the body that does not exist; the miracle solves the problem of the mind's guilt that does not exist. When the miracle looks on guilt, it looks past it to the light, and then the guilt is gone. We see the problem as it is, not the way we have set it up. The way we have set it up demands magic. All the laws Jesus speaks of here are magic. I have a sick body, I go to a doctor. I have a sick relationship or am lonely, I go to another body. I have a sick bank account, I earn money. I have an empty lung, I breathe oxygen. I want what another country possesses, I wage war. All this is magic. Anything that addresses the problem of the body on the level of the world, collectively or individually, is magic. It is important to note that Jesus makes it very clear that magic is not evil and that we should not try to avoid it as long as we think of ourselves as bodies. But we need to be aware that it is magic (T-2.IV.4-5).

(W-pI.76.6:4) What it is meant to save does not exist.

Magic is meant to save a nonexistent body that is not the problem, likewise on the collective level with the world. These simple sentences are very clear and uncomplicated in their message that we should look at the *tiny, mad idea* and laugh, look at all its expressions in our everyday life and laugh—not derisively and not in an attacking way, but because it is so silly to think that anything not of God has power to affect the love in our minds.

If you understand the ego's purpose for the world and the body, this becomes much easier. First understand it intellectually, and over time it will become easier and easier to identify with (see W-pII.284.1). The ego's purpose is to root our attention in the mindless. Period. As long as it succeeds, as it has done remarkably well, the ego remains alive and well, and will forever be alive and well because it exists only by virtue of the mind's belief in it. When the mind withdraws its belief, the ego will disappear because it is nothing. How could the thought of separation from God be anything? But if you believe in it, then in your delusional thinking and hallucinations you will think it is there. Change

105

your mind about it and the ego is gone. What prevents this from happening is the ongoing decision to be mindless.

Therefore, at the same time you are taking care of your bodily needs, physically and psychologically, also be aware that what is really going on is that you are acting out your mind's decision for the ego. You can take care of your body's needs peacefully and lovingly without judgment, or you can take care of them with guilt, anger, and specialness. The body is neutral. Once you decide to get sick, your sickness is neutral. Once you get involved in a relationship for whatever reason, the relationship is neutral. Once you decide to be born, your life here is neutral. Everything then depends on which teacher you use: the teacher of magic or the teacher of miracles.

(W-pI.76.6:5) Only what it is meant to hide will save you.

This is another important line. Once again we are being told that the body was literally made to hide the mind, and only the mind can save us. A paragraph in the text clearly explains the role the body and world play in keeping guilt hidden (T-18.IX.4). Specifically made to keep us unaware of our guilt, the body continues to behave as guilt directs, without our ever knowing what is happening. Even more specifically, the body's sensory organs do not perceive the mind's guilt, but do perceive the world's guilt, and thus seemingly prove its existence in others. Stated another way, the body was made *not* to go within to the mind, but to keep us in a perpetual state of mindlessness.

(W-pI.76.7:1-4) The laws of God [love, eternal life, Oneness] **can never be replaced. We will devote today to rejoicing that this is so. It is no longer a truth that we would hide. We realize instead it is a truth that keeps us free forever.**

Jesus may be a bit optimistic in saying "It is no longer a truth that we would hide." He is assuming that by the time students reach this lesson they would no longer want to use their bodies to hide the mind's truth of Atonement.

The world would bind us. Dostoevsky's underground man knew that the world's laws of $2 + 2 = 4$ imprisoned him and everyone else. That is why I said in my introduction that he is the first existential hero in modern literature. He stands up and says, "I will not be bound by this."

(W-pI.76.7:5) Magic imprisons, but the laws of God make free.

Magic imprisons because it keeps us mindless. This does not mean you should not take aspirin if you have a headache, but that when you do, know what you are doing. Know that you are merely taking care of a symptom that the ego made to keep you rooted in a body. If you are aware of this, you will be reflecting the fact that you have a mind, and so are turning the tables on the ego. If you insist you are not going to take a pill or see a doctor because that is not spiritual, all you are doing is reinforcing the "fact" that the ego is strong. You are not saying it is nonexistent; you are saying your ego is alive and well and you are not going to give it any power. But can you give power to what does not exist? By saying you will not give it any power, you have already given it power. That is why fighting against something is not the answer, echoed in the famous biblical statement, "Resist not evil" (Matthew 5:39).

If you are sick, you obviously think you are a body and this means that you are already in a "fear-weakened state" (T-2.IV.4:8), which is why Jesus speaks of a compromise approach in which magic and miracles are combined. *Magic* refers to whatever medicine or other forms you feel will help you, and the *miracle* refers to being aware of what your mind is doing. Remember, forgiveness "is still, and quietly

108

does nothing. ... It merely looks, and waits, and judges not" (W-pII.1.4:1,3). Do not do anything; do not fight against your ego. Just look and be aware of your mind's decision. Thus, you are never upset for the reason you think (W-pI.5), or sick for the reason you think, and you never get well for the reason you think. If your mind's choosing the ego gave you a headache, then by your mind choosing the Holy Spirit you may very well take an aspirin to get rid of the headache. What heals you is not the aspirin, however, but your mind's decision not to hurt yourself. A section in the teachers' manual specifically addresses this (M-5. II.2), referring to the "special agents" that seem to be ministering to us to make us well, concealing the change of mind that does heal us. Because we think we are bodies, we believe what is making us well is the aspirin because we are too afraid of the mind's power. This fear made us sick in the first place, and we are still too afraid of the mind to reverse its decision, which we are all perfectly capable of doing at any instant.

It is essential to respect your fear and resistance and not fight against them. Do not pretend you are spiritual. If you were you would not be here, so the fact that you are here, let alone sick, is saying you are not as spiritual as you thought. *And that is not a sin*. Forgiving yourself for *not* being spiritual is what will make you spiritual. If you forgive yourself for being born, for having a body and having your body get sick, and you then say, "Well, that is what egos do, and obviously I am too afraid of the truth," at least you are being honest. Then take as many aspirin as you need, or do whatever will lessen the pain. Just don't judge yourself for having a headache or taking an aspirin. Remember, forgiveness "merely looks, and waits, and judges not."

To repeat: "Magic imprisons, but the laws of God make free." They make us free because we reflect those laws by becoming minds instead of bodies. The right mind is a reflection of the One Mind in which everyone is one; therefore, in our right minds we do not judge or exclude. We cannot even say "everyone" as there is only one. But once we judge ourselves, let alone anyone else, we are right back into the ego and its thought system of guilt and hate.

And finally:

(W-pI.76.7:6) The light has come because there are no laws but His.

The light has come because the light is always there. Moreover, it is not that "the light has come," *we come to the light*. The light is the Atonement thought, the Holy Spirit, the memory of God we took with us when we fell asleep. That light reminds us, since there is only God, that there are no laws but His; everything else is made up. To say it one last time, this lesson will make sense only if you read it as a mind (2 + 2 = 5), not as a body (2 + 2 = 4). As you read it as a body, which is inevitable, at least be aware that you are reading it through the lens of your own belief in separation, so of course you are going to misunderstand and distort what the Course teaches.

9. The Reflection of God's Laws in the World

The next few passages will flesh out even more the laws of the world and their underlying premises, and how the laws of God can be reflected here. We begin with the section entitled "The State of Grace."

(T-7.XI.1:1-2) The Holy Spirit will always guide you truly, because your joy is His. This is His Will for everyone because He speaks for the Kingdom of God, which *is* joy.

Of central importance is the statement in the second sentence: "This is His Will for everyone...." The world's laws (2 + 2 = 4) are laws that exclude, dividing the world into winners and losers, good guys and bad guys, victims and victimizers, people who deserve to be punished and killed, and those who are spared. Yet how can this be if the Holy Spirit's Will is for everyone to be joyful? This would immediately put us in opposition to Him because we do not want joy for *everyone*. We do not want joy for the bad people in our families and places of work, let alone in the world. There have to be those we can label as sinful so we can project our unconscious guilt onto them, and so we do not will joy for them. In fact, we cannot will joy for them because of the ego's law of *one or the other*: If they are joyful, I am not; but if I am joyful, they are not. Therefore, I want to see to it that they are miserable. We project our guilt onto them, seeing in them our "secret sins and hidden hates" (T-31.VIII.9:2), and then we attack in them what we have projected. We will make them joy-*less*, and this, again, means that we are joyful, which directly opposes the Holy Spirit's purpose. And this makes our egos joyful indeed!

(T-7.XI.1:3) Following Him is therefore the easiest thing in the world, and the only thing that is easy, because it is not of the world.

It is hard work to live in the world because we always have to adjust to its insanity. We have to adjust to a world where $2 + 2 = 4$, when it is not that way at all. We have to adjust to a world that is a projection of the equally insane thought that $1 + 1 = 2$. The truth remains, however, that $1 + 1 = 1$: God's Son has never been separate from his Source. Since the Sonship is one, everyone who seems to be separate is also one. But the world says just the opposite. Everyone is separate from everyone else: $2 + 2 = 4$, and it can be proven by what science says. It can be proven that bodies are separate, that there are evil people who do evil things. These are the world's laws, which go against the only natural law there is, Heaven's perfect Oneness.

Within the dream, the law of perfect Oneness is reflected in our being perfectly the same: the same wrong mind, right mind, and decision maker. Accepting that is easy because it is the truth. Anything else is difficult, for it would be fighting against the truth, which takes tremendous effort. This is one way of understanding why we need to sleep at night, for we are exhausted from the effort of trying all day to prove that $2 + 2 = 4$, trying to prove that the unnatural state of existence is natural, while our natural state of spirit is unnatural.

(T-7.XI.1:4-5) It is therefore natural. The world goes against your nature, being out of accord with God's laws.

Our nature is that we are a Child of God, one with our Creator and one with everyone else. We are innocent and unseparated, even though it seems otherwise, because we have ended up as guilty/ angry and mindless puppets who think they have a self and brain of their own where they can actually choose what they would do. Once we identify with the puppet, it makes no sense to speak of oneness as a natural state. What has become natural is $2 + 2$

equaling 4. This means things are set and lawful here, and very real.

(T-7.XI.1:6-8) The world perceives orders of difficulty in everything. This is because the ego perceives nothing as wholly desirable. By demonstrating to yourself there is no order of difficulty in miracles, you will convince yourself that, in your natural state, there is no difficulty at all *because* it is a state of grace.

In this context "grace" refers to our reality as spirit, which is the only natural state. The ego perceives *orders of difficulty* in everything, a more primitive way of saying *there is a hierarchy of illusions* (our familiar first law of chaos): some problems are easier or more difficult to solve than others. And so the 2 + 2 = 4 world of differences is real and governed by the immutable laws of birth, life, and death These laws seem to be beyond our control because we conveniently forget it is our dream. How can you say you are not responsible for what you dream at night when it is your dream? But speaking of our waking dreams, the world tells us we are the effect and not the cause.

The world says that it is part of the natural law that science helps us to discover and understand, enabling us to predict, manipulate, and control what happens here. But nothing really happens here! We think science leads to greater understanding, but we understand nothing. There is *no order of difficulty in miracles* because everything here is the same. There is one problem: choosing the ego's thought system of separation. There is one solution: choosing the Holy Spirit's thought system of Atonement. There is nothing in between.

The first principle of miracles states that "There is no order of difficulty in miracles. One is not 'harder' or 'bigger' than another. They are all the same. All expressions of love are maximal" (T-1.I.1). If we truly understood this, we would not have to read anything else in the book. It does not appear that every problem is the same, but remember that the world lies, having been made to deceive us. Its purpose is to tell us there *is* a world, for which the body was made as well. Restating this, the world and body were made to convince us that our natural state is mindlessness. Of course, they do not tell us this because *mindlessness* implies there once was a mind and now it is gone. The ego does not even use the word *mindless* because it does not use the word *mind*, not recognizing its existence.

When egos talk about the mind they really are talking about the brain. The mind becomes this quasi-mystical, something-or-other activity of the brain that is integral to the body's world of $2 + 2 = 4$. Programmed by the mind, the brain analyzes the data brought to it by the body's elaborate sensory apparatus, concluding that there is a world out there, replete with people and problems: a hierarchy of difficulty and therefore a hierarchy of solutions. Thus, in this insanity it is more challenging to heal cancer than to heal a headache, hangnail, or splinter. Yet they are all the same because they all make the body real, a fact that underlies the statement: "While you believe that it [the body] can give you pleasure, you will also believe that it can bring you pain" (T-19.IV-A.17:11). Both pleasure and pain give reality to the body, reinforcing our mindlessness. We therefore experience love in this world as between two bodies, whether it be familial, friendship, romantic, or sexual. Love here is always between bodies, which means the relationship is not love because it is not of the mind. Consequently, the world is always wrong about everything. $2 + 2 = 5$!

Continuing our theme, we turn to two paragraphs from "Salvation from Fear" in Chapter 24:

(T-24.VI.4:1-2) Forget not that the healing of God's Son is all the world is for. That is the only purpose the Holy Spirit sees in it, and thus the only one it has.

"The healing of God's Son" is the only purpose for the world. Once it was made by the ego as a way of keeping us separate from God and preventing us from returning home, the world became neutral. The Holy Spirit's purpose for the world is that it be a classroom in which we learn to heal our minds. It is not the body that needs healing, or social institutions that have to be changed, but the mind, especially if it believes there are problems in the world that require healing, whether they be medical, economic, political, or social.

If the healing takes place in the mind and that is the only purpose the Holy Spirit sees, He must be in the mind too. Since He does not see anything external to the mind, there not being anything there, it makes no sense to ask His help to solve problems here. The world is nothing more than a projection of an illusory thought that never leaves its source in the mind. Why, then, would the Holy Spirit help you with a world and problems that are not there? Rather, He helps you change the mind's *decision* for the illusion that does heal God's Son. He does not overthrow the laws of the world, nor ask you to overthrow them. He simply asks you to smile gently at them and say: "What laws of the world? What do they have to do with me? I know two plus two is five, so how can the two-plus-two-is-four world affect my peace?" You do not rebel or fight against the world, or seek to overthrow it, but—again—you recognize that the world has nothing to do with your mind. The self that believes this is the decision-making mind that has become right-minded. We are told that the world is an "outside picture of an inward condition" (T-21.in.1:5) and that perception is "the outward picture of a wish; an image that you wanted to be true" (T-24.VII.8:10). The world therefore is the out-picturing or projection of the mind's unconscious wish that we be separate, innocent, and not responsible for the separation, meaning someone else will pay the price for our perceived sin.

This, then, is the nature of the help we are given by Jesus, the Holy Spirit, and *A Course in Miracles*. They help us look differently at our bodies and their relationships with other bodies. We learn that we are not victims of other people, beginning with our parents. That is the world's big myth, and one the ego fosters. We cannot be children of our parents because we are not bodies. Regardless of what our parents did or did not do, our past has nothing to do with our minds. Sure it made a difference to us when we were young, but unless we want to remain spiritual children, what possible difference can it make to us now? Of course our parents had egos, and we know that egos are vicious and ripe with specialness. But why do we have to let another's ego affect us? All our relationships, regardless of their form, are projections of the mind's decision for its teacher. We are taught that the only relationship that is meaningful is our mind's relationship with the Holy Spirit, reflecting our real relationship with God (T-15.VIII).

From the love that comes from joining with the Holy Spirit, all relationships here will be blessed— loving, caring, and kind—and they will be role specific. This means that we do what the role intends: be kind to our parents, even though, as minds, we know they are not our parents; we will be kind to friends, lovers, spouses, and children, despite these relationships being projections or extensions of the mind's relationship with the ego or the Holy Spirit. We are freed, then, to be loving and caring to everyone, appropriate to the form of the relationship, which makes all our relationships easy and natural. We begin at the source, the decision maker's choice for its teacher, and then recognize the effects of that choice. If they are painful, we know we chose the ego; if they are peaceful and we embrace everyone in that peace, we know we chose the Holy Spirit. How much simpler can life here be?

(T-24.VI.4:3) Until you see the healing of the Son as all you wish to be accomplished by the world, by time and all appearances, you will not know the Father nor yourself.

The key to understanding why this is so is to recognize and accept that the Son is everyone. If you do not see your purpose in the world as the healing of *all* the spots of darkness in your mind, which would exclude people or groups from the circle of Atonement, you will never know the Father or yourself. Who is the Father? Perfect Oneness. Who is your Self? God's perfect and one Son. But if you are afraid of God's Love and Oneness, you will dedicate yourself to *not* healing God's Son. You will live a life of despair, anger, resentment, hurt, sickness, guilt, anxiety, pain, alienation, and on and on. And the ego jumps for joy over each one of them.

Jesus is asking us to have the vision that sees everyone as the same. This means that no perception of anger is ever justified. When we are angry, we need to forgive ourselves for projecting our fear onto some other person or group. What makes this course difficult to practice is that we are asked to include everyone, not just certain people— strangers as well as intimates in our lives. The world's purpose is "the healing of God's Son," and God's Son is one. $2 + 2 = 5$, not 4. The world does not tell the truth. In its thinking, and in the thinking of most religions, God does not welcome everyone home—only His chosen people, the good people. Sinners go to hell. That, of course, explains why the Bible has been and continues to be such an incredibly popular book. It justifies all our perceptions of judgment, hatred, and anger. If God can judge and hate, then by God I can too! And not only that, I can invoke God to support me. But if we see the world's only purpose as the healing of God's Son, and we recognize God's Son is one, then everything we do, think, and say has to come from the content of love that embraces everyone without exception. Our function, then, is to forgive ourselves for not doing that. "Everyone without exception" includes ourselves, as well as everyone else. That "without exception" is what makes this course so difficult.

(T-24.VI.4:4) For you will use the world for what is not its purpose, and will not escape its laws of violence and death.

If you do not use the world for its true purpose, you will see it only as a way of meeting your needs. To the Holy Spirit , the world's purpose is to be a classroom in which we learn "I am God's Son." Therefore, to attack anyone is to attack myself because God's Son is one. When we do not use the world for this purpose, we will not escape the world's laws of violence and death. If we see ourselves as a victim of these vicious laws, it is only because we put ourselves under those laws. And *that* is the problem.

Near the end of Chapter 27 we read: "Let them be as hateful and as vicious as they may, they could have no effect on you unless you failed to recognize it is your dream" (T-27.VIII.10:6). Even if the figures in the dream that is your life are hatefully vicious, the only way they can have an effect on you is if you have forgotten this is your dream. When you realize it, how can it bother you? When you are asleep at night, having a terrible dream yet are a lucid dreamer, which means while still asleep you know you are dreaming, you will not be afraid because you know it is all happening in a dream. And so Jesus is helping us become lucid dreamers in the waking dreams we call life.

While we believe we are here, Jesus wants us to be aware that our lives are taking place within a dream. "Let them be as hateful and as vicious as they may, they can have no effect on you unless you failed to recognize it is your dream." When you let the world diminish you, infuriate you, get you down, or cause you to become depressed and despairing, it is only because you forgot this is a dream. If you are in any state of disquiet, you must have wanted it because it is your dream, your secret wish. Recall that perception is the mind's wish projected out. This puts full responsibility on us for everything we feel. We usually cannot stop others from attacking us, physically or verbally, anymore than we can stop the radiating and polluting of the atmosphere, water, and soil, but that is only on the level of the dream. If we are not in the dream, what difference does any of this make? As Jesus says of the miracle: "The miracle establishes you dream a dream, and that its content is not true" (T-28.II.7:1).

Think of the movie *The Matrix*. If you are not in the matrix, what goes on in it does not hurt you, which means you are not justified in blaming anyone or anything for what you feel. It is your dream. A major illusion of the world is that bodies feel. But how can that be? A puppet does not feel anything. Feelings are projected thoughts from the mind, and there are only two constellations of thoughts: guilt and fear, forgiveness and love. What the body feels has been given it to feel by the mind, which means it is the mind that is the problem if you do not like what you are feeling. Our experience to the contrary, bodies lie. $2 + 2 = 4$ only in the dream. If someone hits you and your arm gets black and blue, it is not because the person hit you. It is black and blue because you chose to be in a body under the body's laws that dictate if someone punches you in the arm, you will get black and blue. So your arm is sore, and in your insanity, you will think someone did that to you, which is perfectly true within the dream. But why do you want to give reality to a dream? That is the question we always need to ask ourselves, preferably before we act.

(T-24.VI.4:5) Yet it is given you to be beyond its laws in all respects, in every way and every circumstance, in all temptation to perceive what is not there, and all belief God's Son can suffer pain because he sees himself as he is not.

God's Son suffers pain because he sees himself as a body. He sees himself as a body because he *wants* to see himself that way, for two reasons. The first is that it establishes that he exists as a separate self. Second, he exists but it is not his fault, because another body that followed the world's laws did this to him. A psychological law says that the child is father of the man: what happens to you as a child will affect you when you are an adult; being abused as a child, for example, will color all your later experiences. But this law is true only if you are a body. If you know you are an atemporal mind, you can step outside your past as easily as you change clothes. You cannot be affected by a past that does not exist. Only if you believe you can be affected by it will it affect you. This does not mean that you deny your ego's interpretation of what you are feeling, only that you not justify the ego's lies.

To repeat this long and important sentence: "Yet it is given you to be beyond its laws in all respects, in every way and every circumstance, in all temptation to perceive what is not there…" It is within our power as minds to choose not to be bound by the world's laws, not to be bound by $2 + 2 = 4$. We can be at peace regardless of what goes on in the body—our own, the bodies of loved ones, or the world at large.

Once again, this state of inner peace is independent of outer circumstances. There have been many reports of people in death camps and the like being models of forgiveness and peace, even while tortured and their deaths imminent.

Students will never truly progress in this course as long as they think it is about the body and personality they think they are. *A Course in Miracles* uses those self-perceptions to lead us beyond them, so we will realize it is written from a mind to a mind. We are not bodies; God is not a body; the Holy Spirit is not a body; Jesus is not a body; and forgiveness does not occur between bodies.

(T-24.VI.5:1) Look on your brother and behold in him the whole reversal of the laws that seem to rule this world.

Jesus is telling us to look on this special love or special hate partner, and if we see through his gentle eyes, we will see "the whole reversal of the laws that seem to rule this world." These are the laws of *one or the other*; someone wins, another loses. If I establish you as sinful, I am sinless because it is *one or the other*, part of the more basic law that $2 + 2 = 4$. I prove you are the evildoer, bring you to justice, and I am off the hook. Because God now knows—I have told Him

128

you are the bad one—you get punished, which means I am saved. This *is* how the world works. Jesus' law of correction, however, is the law of "together, or not at all" (T-19.IV-D.12:8). In my mind—meaning *content*, not *form* or behavior—either you and I go home together, or neither of us does. This reflects Heaven's "Oneness joined as One" (T-25.I.7:1), and is the meaning of Jesus' above sentence.

(T-24.VI.5:2) See in his freedom yours, for such it is.

If you free him, you are free, because you and your brother are alike. It is not true that if he is sinful, you are sinless, because that makes you different. If you see him as sinful, you see yourself as sinful too, because $2 + 2 = 5$. The ego's $2 + 2 = 4$ means there are differences. Everything in this world is predicated on differences. Jesus' law is that we are all the same. If I make you sinful, I am condemning myself, and since God's Son is one, I am also condemning Jesus. I am condemning everyone, both the people I think I hate and the people I think I love, and that is what I have to look at. Even a mild twinge of annoyance is driving another nail into Jesus' body and everyone else's. We have to stop and ask ourselves whether this is really what we want. Succinctly stated, the ego's law is one of differences; Jesus' law is that we are the same. It is very simple.

(T-24.VI.5:3-4) Let not his specialness obscure the truth in him, for not one law of death you bind him to will you escape. And not one sin you see in him but keeps you both in hell.

If I see it in you, I see it in me. So your brother has specialness in him, what does that have to do with you or him? Sure he has specialness. He has a wrong mind. You have specialness. You have a wrong mind. Everyone has a wrong mind. What's the big deal? Everyone has an ego; everyone has a right mind. But we like to point out that certain people have evil wrong minds because we believe there is a hierarchy of wrongness. We follow the world's laws of differences, but we are not different. We are the same.

(T-24.VI.5:5) Yet will his perfect sinlessness release you both [if you see him as sinless, you have to be sinless], **for holiness is quite impartial, with one judgment made for all it looks upon.**

All it looks upon. Underline the word *all*. Everything holiness looks upon is seen as the same. It is impartial because everyone is the same. Recall the Course's word play on *partial:* Vision is impartial because it is not prejudiced and does not have biases. It is also impartial because it does not see in parts. The Sonship of God is one.

(T-24.VI.5:6) And that [one judgment] **is made, not of itself, but through the Voice that speaks for God in everything that lives and shares His Being.**

Everything lives and shares His Being, both what we think of as animate and inanimate. Everything comes from thought, and there is only one thought. We are all part of that one thought, united with the Thought that is our Source. Thus, the bottom line in terms of practicing *A Course in Miracles* is to be vigilant for how we want to make the law of differentiation the law of reality. The reality of differences is sanity from the world's point of view. We simply do not want to see everyone and everything as the same. $2 + 2 = 5$ is anathema to us.

A few sentences from "The Special Function" nicely round out our discussion:

(T-25.VI.5:1) Here, where the laws of God do not prevail in perfect form, can he yet do *one* perfect thing and make *one* perfect choice.

If "the laws of God do not prevail in perfect form," they do not prevail at all, except in reflection. In this world of multiplicity, separation, attack, and differences, we can still do one perfect thing: forgive.

(T-25.VI.5:2-6) And by this act of special faithfulness to one perceived as other than himself, he learns the gift was given to himself, and so they must be one. Forgiveness is the only function meaningful in time. It is the means the Holy Spirit uses to translate specialness from sin into salvation. Forgiveness is for all. But when it rests on all it is complete, and every function of this world completed with it.

That is our purpose in being here: to heal God's *one* Son. Forgiveness is the Course's name for that process of healing, which means we must learn that everyone is the same and not different, and that if we attack, criticize, or mock one person, we are mocking everyone ("Forgiveness is for all"; *not some*). This makes sense only when we look at it from the perspective of the mind: bodies are good and bad— there are those that do terrible things and those that suffer from these attacks, and there are bodies that do good things. But bodies come from the mind, and everyone's mind is the same. This reverses the laws of the world and leads us from $2 + 2 = 4$ to $2 + 2 = 5$. From there we look at the ego's original thought of $1 + 1 = 2$, and finally to the place where we see the entirety of the dream and its falsity, remembering that $1 + 1$ is still, and always will be, 1.

10. One Plus One Equals One

Lesson 329, "I have already chosen what You will," wonderfully summarizes the goal of remembering that $1 + 1 = 1$: reality is our oneness with each other and with God—"a Oneness joined as One" (T-25.I.7:1). In reading these words we realize its truth—our truth— and remember that the way to know this truth is the daily practice of learning its reflection here. This is the process of forgiveness that reflects Heaven's perfect Oneness: we are all the same—attacking one person attacks all; totally forgiving one person forgives all.

Part II of the workbook consists of lovely prayers such as the one in this lesson. There are usually two parts to each lesson. One is a prayer we say to God, and the other is something we say to each other, or in this case, Jesus says to us. The order is reversed in different lessons. Here, the beginning is the prayer we say to our Father, and then the close is Jesus' words to us. Do recall that these prayers are metaphorical, as the one true God cannot hear or understand words that are part of the dualistic universe. But these lovely words reflect our prayers to ourselves, that we remember that $1 + 1 = 1$, and that we remain as God

created us: His perfect and undivided Son, united in
His Will of Love.

Lesson 329
I have already chosen what You will.

*Father, I thought I wandered from Your Will,
defied it, broke its laws, and interposed a second will
more powerful than Yours. Yet what I am in truth is
but Your Will, extended and extending. This am I,
and this will never change. As You are One, so am I
one with You. And this I chose in my creation, where
my will became forever one with Yours. That choice
was made for all eternity. It cannot change, and be
in opposition to itself. Father, my will is Yours. And
I am safe, untroubled and serene, in endless joy,
because it is Your Will that it be so.*

Today we will accept our union with each other
and our Source. We have no will apart from His, and
all of us are one because His Will is shared by all of
us. Through it we recognize that we are one. Through
it we find our way at last to God.

APPENDIX

THE WORLD OF 2 + 2 = 5

("The Lighthouse" • Volume 17 Number 2 June 2006)

Kenneth Wapnick, Ph.D.

Introduction

Last year I gave a workshop entitled "When 2 + 2 = 5,"[1] which contrasted the ego's world of 2 + 2 = 4 with the 2 + 2 = 5 world offered us by Jesus. The current article expands on certain themes from that class.

The inspiration for the workshop, and therefore this article, comes from Dostoevsky's seminal *Notes from Underground*, which could be described in part as the spiritual father of modern existentialism. The heirs include men of the stature of Nietzsche, Freud, and Camus. Dostoevsky's hero, if one can use that epithet for such a tormented and angry, though insightful soul, is the mouthpiece for the Russian author's views on becoming free of society's constraints—the world in which we are imprisoned by the rigid laws of 2 + 2 = 4. As the rebellious Underground Man states:

---

1. Available in CD (#117).

"For goodness sakes," they'll yell at you, "you can't rebel, this is two times two makes four... "Good Lord, what do I care about the laws of nature and arithmetic, if for some reason I don't like those laws and this two times two makes four....Oh absurdity of all absurdities!...what kind of will of one's own is that going to be, when things come to tables and arithmetic, when there will be only two times two makes four around? My will or not, two times two would still be four.... an insufferable thing. Two times two makes four is, in my opinion, nothing but an impertinence, yes, sir. Two times two makes four looks like a dandy, struts like a cock of the walk blocking your way, and spits. I agree that two times two makes four is a wonderful thing; but if we are to praise everything, then two times two makes five is sometimes a most delightful little thing.[2]

Indeed, $2 + 2 = 5$[3] is a *most delightful little thing*, since it reflects the Holy Spirit's correction for the ego's laws of separation and specialness. Thus, the world of $2 + 2 = 4$ reflects the external world of seeming certainty, the ego's world of the body and

2. NY: Thomas Y. Crowell Company, 1969; pp. 12f, 31, 33.

3. While Dostoevsky writes, two times two makes four or five, I have adopted the more conventional expression, two plus two equals four or five.

its laws, what the ancient Gnostics called *archons* or *world rulers*. Yes, we exist here, the Underground Man would state, but our heart and soul are elsewhere, in the world of 2 + 2 = 5, what *A Course in Miracles* means by the right mind that exists outside time and space.

But let us return to the Beginning, without which one cannot understand the ego's thought system and the significance of 2 + 2 = 5, the Holy Spirit's correction for the ego's material world of 2 + 2 = 4.

One Mind: 1 + 1 = 1

Heaven—the true reality—is a state of perfect Oneness in which God and His one creation dwell as one, for such they are:

> The Kingdom of Heaven is the dwelling place of the Son of God, who left not his Father and dwells not apart from Him. Heaven is not a place nor a condition. It is merely an awareness of perfect Oneness, and the knowledge that there is nothing else; nothing outside this Oneness, and nothing else within (T-18.VI.1:4-6).

This means that though we speak of one God and His one Son, in truth there is only the One. Even the Trinity—Father, Son (Christ), and Holy Spirit—is a set of symbols, for there *is* no differentiation or distinction within the Godhead of truth. Thus Jesus teaches us:

> The first in time means nothing, but the First in eternity is God the Father, Who is both First and One. Beyond the First there is no other, for there is no order, no second or third, and nothing but the First (T-14.IV.1:7-8).

In other words, in God's living Oneness there is no Father and Son, and so 1 + 1 = 1. Of such undifferentiated unity is truly the Kingdom of Heaven:

> As it [love] is one itself, it looks on all as one. Its meaning lies in oneness. And it must elude the mind that thinks of it as partial or in part....Love is a law without an opposite. Its wholeness is the power holding everything as one, the link between the Father and the Son which holds Them Both forever as the same (W-pI.127.3:2-4,7-8).

Or, as the text says: we are a "Oneness joined as One" (T-25.I.7:1).

And then something *seemed* to happen—the "tiny, mad idea" or the original error.

142

The Original Error: 1 + 1 = 2
The Secret Dream

> Into eternity, where all is one, there crept a tiny, mad idea, at which the Son of God remembered not to laugh. In his forgetting did the thought become a serious idea, and possible of both accomplishment and real effects (T-27.VIII.6:2-3).

The language of myth allows us to describe what appeared to shatter the pristine unity of reality. It was as if God's Son suddenly decided he was other than perfect Oneness, with an identity that established him as an independent entity, transforming oneness into separation from his Source, the primordial world of 1 + 1 = 2 in which he selfishly exists solely for himself, without concern for the Other.

This is how *A Course in Miracles* describes the original error, when separation took the place of unity, fragmentation substituted for wholeness, and the ego usurped God's role on the throne of creation:

> First, you believe that what God created can be changed by your own mind.

> Second, you believe that what is perfect can be rendered imperfect or lacking.

143

Third, you believe that you can distort the creations of God, including yourself.

Fourth, you believe that you can create yourself, and that the direction of your own creation is up to you.

These related distortions represent a picture of what actually occurred in the separation, or the "detour into fear" (T-2.I.1:9-2:1).

Once the tiny, mad idea of separation—the Son's Declaration of Independence—seemed to occur, it was if a state of war were declared, for in the world of undifferentiated unity the concept of an individual entity has no place. Thus, in order to exist, the Son of God had to dispose of oneness, turning his Creator into an enemy who would never rest until His Son's sin was avenged:

> "You have usurped the place of God. Think not He has forgotten."… An angry father pursues his guilty son. Kill or be killed….The stain of blood can never be removed, and anyone who bears this stain on him must meet with death (M-17.7:3-4,10-11,13).

The "detour into fear" is actually a detour into sin, guilt, and fear; the last being the inevitable result of the first two. The ego convinced us that the separation was, in fact, an attack on God (*sin*), for which we should feel unredeemable remorse and self-hatred (*guilt*), deserving the ultimate punishment (which we *fear*). The non-dualistic reality of $1 + 1 = 1$ was thus destroyed, and in its place arose the ego's heaven of $1 + 1 = 2$, ruled by the dualistic god of the ego's world, at war with his sinful and usurping offspring. To escape annihilation at the hands of this made-up deity, the ego counseled the terrified Son—really the separated Son speaking to himself—to leave his mind and make up a world and body in which to hide, thus preserving his newly-won self. In that "first projection of error outward" (T-18.I.6:1), the one Son of separation became fragmented into billions and billions of seemingly separated selves, each one housed in forms or bodies. As Jesus explains:

> You who believe that God is fear made but one substitution. It has taken many forms, because it was the substitution of illusion for truth; of fragmentation for wholeness. It has become so splintered and subdivided and divided again, over and over, that it is now almost impossible to perceive it once was one, and still is what it was. That one error, which brought truth to illusion, infinity to time, and life to death, was all you ever

made. Your whole world rests upon it. Everything
you see reflects it, and every special relationship
that you have ever made is part of it (T-18.I.4).

Therefore, once the separation occurred and
the tiny, mad idea was accorded reality, $1 + 1 = 2$
became the truth, and $1 + 1 = 1$ the illusion. The
ego's distortions of $1 + 1 = 1$ can be likened to two
dreams: the mind's secret dream of separation and
usurpation, and the world's dream of specialness
and victimization—the first involves only the mind,
while the second centers on the body to the absolute
exclusion of the mind. *The Gifts of God*—the prose
poem taken down by the Course's scribe, Helen
Schucman— cogently describes these two dreams,
both based on the fear that is born of the belief in the
separation from God:

> So fear was made, and with it came the need
> for gifts [the second dream] to lend the substance
> to a dream [the first dream] in which there is no
> substance. Now the dream seems to have value,
> for its offerings appear as hope and strength and
> even love, if only for an instant. They content
> the frightened dreamer for a little while, and let
> him not remember the first dream which gifts of
> fear but offer him again. The seeming solace of
> illusions' gifts are now his armor, and the sword

he holds to save himself from waking. For before he could awaken, he would first be forced to call to mind the first dream once again....Yet if he thinks that he must first go through a greater terror still, he must see hope in what will now appear the "better" dream (*The Gifts of God*, p. 120).

Thus does the ego warn us of the ultimate penalty for violating its laws, and, fearing the worst—our annihilation—we pledge ourselves to its lawful world of special relationships, "the better world" of 2 + 2 = 4: the externalization of the ego's inner world of 1 + 1 = 2.

The Wrong-Minded World of Special Relationships: 2 + 2 = 4
The Ego's Nightmare Dream of Separate Interests

The ego's world of 2 + 2 = 4 is the world we know. It follows specific laws and is regulated by adherence to form (the world and body), always at the expense of content (the mind). In this world, 2 plus 2 always equals 4, for the laws of mathematics are immutable. In a world governed by perception this is absolute truth. Since the Holy Spirit, the Voice of reason, has been excluded from awareness, the only voice we know is the ego's, and the only laws we obey are its own. This accords the ego the authority of a god, and so its very words become gospel truth. To breach them means punishment and ostracism, which explains why the majority of the population identifies with the status quo and is loathe to go against society's (i.e., the ego's) dictates and mores. Thus are we asked to compromise and sacrifice the truth in our minds, and live in a world of finite and certain exactitude, slaves to inexorable laws that are mere expanded shadows of the ego's seemingly immutable law of separation: $1 + 1 = 2$.

In Lesson 76, "I am under no laws but God's," Jesus underscores the same thoughts by poking fun at the world's laws that we hold so dear:

> We have observed before how many senseless things have seemed to you to be salvation. Each has imprisoned you with laws as senseless as itself. You are not bound by them....Think of the freedom in the recognition that you are not bound by all the strange and twisted laws you have set up to save you. You really think that you would starve unless you have stacks of green paper strips and piles of metal discs. You really think a small round pellet or some fluid pushed into your veins

> through a sharpened needle will ward off disease
> and death. You really think you are alone unless
> another body is with you....These are not laws,
> but madness (W-pI.76.1:1-3; 3; 5:1).

This, of course, makes absolutely no sense to us who
identify so completely with our bodies—physically
and psychologically. How can we exist without
money to pay for food and shelter; how would it
be possible to survive disease without some sort of
medical intervention; and how could anyone live
happily in this world without companionship? Yet we
know the world is insane, seeing and hearing what is
not there, denying the love that is our Self. Indeed,
such denial *is* the ego's purpose for making the world:

> No law the world obeys can help you grasp
> love's meaning. What the world believes was
> made to hide love's meaning, and to keep it dark
> and secret. There is not one principle the world
> upholds but violates the truth of what love is, and
> what you are as well (W-pI.127.5).

The certainty that the ego puts forth to obscure
love's meaning finds its home in the special
relationship. Within its guilt-centered and hate-
infested confines the Son of God finds the love the ego
has promised him. This shadow world but manifests

the ego's original sin of selfishness, wherein we sacrifice another—originally God and His Son—to the demands of our need for self-preservation. Since the ego's means of survival is the principle of *one or the other*, listening to its voice, as we must, means we have no recourse but to follow its harsh dictates. Our lives therefore but mirror our origin: obedience to the law of *separate interests*—the law of $1 + 1 = 2$.

In the world of $2 + 2 = 4$, we actually think we know what is best for us, for we use our past experience in the world, or the "wisdom" of others as our guide for decision. *A Course in Miracles* continually reminds us of this, and in Lesson 24, "I do not perceive my own best interests," we read:

> In no situation that arises do you realize the outcome that would make you happy. Therefore, you have no guide to appropriate action, and no way of judging the result. What you do is determined by your perception of the situation, and that perception is wrong. It is inevitable, then, that you will not serve your own best interests (W-pI.24.1:1-4).

Moreover, we also believe we can make cogent judgments about ourselves, others, and the world; that we know what is right and wrong, good and bad, healthy or unhealthy. Yet, given our limited information and understanding of the true nature of the body, and our total ignorance of the mind and its causative role, how could we possibly know? Only the arrogance of the ego's thought system of $2 + 2 = 4$ could lead us to such an insane conclusion about our ability:

> The aim of our curriculum, unlike the goal of the world's learning, is the recognition that judgment in the usual sense is impossible. This is not an opinion but a fact. In order to judge anything rightly, one would have to be fully aware of an inconceivably wide range of things; past, present and to come. One would have to recognize in advance all the effects of his judgments on everyone and everything involved in them in any way. And one would have to be certain there is no distortion in his perception, so that his judgment would be wholly fair to everyone on whom it rests now and in the future. Who is in a position to do this? Who except in grandiose fantasies would claim this for himself?
>
> Remember how many times you thought you knew all the "facts" you needed for judgment, and how wrong you were! Is there anyone who has not had this experience? Would you know how many

times you merely thought you were right, without
ever realizing you were wrong? (M-10.3:1-4:3)

Jesus tells us in the text that "nothing [is] so
blinding as perception of form" (T-22.III.6:7), and
yet it is always our past and present perceptions that
we use to determine what is best for us and for others.
And we never recognize that our perceptions are
dictated solely by the mind's unconscious guilt, and
ultimately have nothing to do with what appears to be
objective reality.

Another example of our arrogant ignorance—
Socrates was quoted by Plato as saying that he was
the wisest of men because he knew he did not know
anything—is our belief that we understand the causes
of pain and suffering. Whether it is the physical
and mental pain all people feel, or global issues of
suffering, our egos would have us think that we know
their causes, be they medical, psychological, social,
educational, economic, political, or astronomic. In
other words, the causes of pain can always be found
in the world of $2 + 2 = 4$, the world of science. And so
we will *always* be wrong since there is no world out
there to be causative, any more than there is a world
that can have effects:

> The world is nothing in itself. Your mind
> must give it meaning....There is no world
> apart from what you wish, and herein lies your
> ultimate release....There is no world! This is
> the central thought the course attempts to teach
> (W-pI.132.4:1-2; 5:1; 6:2-3).

What, then, is there to change or heal; what, then, is
there to be studied and understood? Thus Jesus says to
us, in words that only the arrogantly ignorant would
find offensive:

> ...it is very hard for you to realize it is not
> personally insulting that your contribution and the
> Holy Spirit's are so extremely disproportionate.
> You are still convinced that your understanding is
> a powerful contribution to the truth, and makes it
> what it is. Yet we have emphasized that you need
> understand nothing (T-18.IV.7:4-6).

Indeed, we need understand nothing because we *can*
understand nothing. Since brains do not think, they
cannot understand. As the wise fox told St. Exupery's
little prince: "It is only with the heart that one can
see rightly; what is essential is invisible to the eye."
What is essential is the mind, and it is only through
Hamlet's *mind's eye* that we can truly understand the
cause of suffering:

> Once you were unaware of what the cause of
> everything the world appeared to thrust upon you,
> uninvited and unasked, must really be. Of one
> thing you were sure: Of all the many causes you
> perceived as bringing pain and suffering to you,
> your guilt was not among them (T-27.VII.7:3-4).

Without awareness of the mind's guilt, however, we cannot sanely address our problems, and certainly cannot accept their solution. Thus, we have recourse only to the insanity of the ego, which tells us in no uncertain terms that if we follow its guidance we shall find the love, comfort, and peace we sought from God, but were denied. What God could not give, this *special* person with these *special* attributes can. What drives the special relationship is the law of guilt: make others guilty and you will get them to give you what you want—love, attention, high grades, approval, and pity. Make no mistake, this is the law that drives the world and all its relationships—personal and collective. People, groups, and nations are of no significance to us *other than* in their ability to meet our *special* needs. When they do so and have nothing left to give, they are discarded and others found who will do just as nicely—"another can be found" (W-pI.170.8:7). Our interests are our own, and those of others are sacrificed to satisfy them. Whether we pretend to love or hate people outright, they exist nonetheless as specific objects of our projected guilt. When our needs are met by these special partners, we love them; when they are rejected, we hate them: the harsh though simple law of *separate interests*. Paraphrasing the Course, we can say that these ego laws are fool-proof and cannot be broken, changed, or gone beyond; yet they are not God-proof (T-5.VI.10:6).

It is Jesus' purpose in his course to help us loosen—gradually and gently—the identification with the thought system of insanity so we can remember there is a sane law in the mind that transcends the ego's seemingly immutable laws and helps us remember we are mind, and mind alone. When we call upon God's Voice for help, we are answered by the Holy Spirit's law of 2 + 2 = 5—the law of forgiveness that tells us we forgive others for what they have *not* done to us; from the world's perspective, a law of non-sense if there ever were one!

The Right-Minded World of
Holy Relationships: 2 + 2 = 5
The Holy Spirit's Forgiving Dream of
Shared Interests

Our big temptation is to believe in the world and its laws. Indeed, the body itself was made to be the medium of such belief, for it was constructed—its sensory apparatus, neuro-logical innervations, and brain—specifically to witness to the reality and power of the world around us, and the sacrosanct nature of its laws. After all, it is the brain that processes the sensory input from the world and concludes that $2 + 2 = 4$, just as a computer operates solely according to the programming of its programmer—change the program and the computer operates differently. Yet there will be no incentive to change the program as long as we believe that it works. And so we do not seek to change our programming until we reach the point of recognition that our lives have failed, realizing on some level that we are being imprisoned by a programmed mind (or will) that we experience to be not our own:

> An imprisoned will engenders a situation which, in the extreme, becomes altogether intolerable.

> Tolerance for pain may be high, but it is not
> without limit. Eventually everyone begins to
> recognize, however dimly, that there *must* be a
> better way. As this recognition becomes more
> firmly established, it becomes a turning point.
> This ultimately reawakens spiritual vision,
> simultaneously weakening the investment in
> physical sight (T-2.III.3:4-8).

This turning point is the shift from the ego's
perception of separation, separate interests, and
laws that bind our minds, to Jesus' vision of shared
interests that points to Heaven's Oneness and the laws
of God. The miracle's purpose is nothing less than to
bring about the shift from the body to the mind:

> The miracle is the first step in giving back to
> cause the function of causation, not effect. For
> this confusion has produced the dream, and while
> it lasts will wakening be feared (T-28.II.9:3-4).

Thus does the miracle return our attention from the
bodily world of *effect* to the mind's world of *cause*;
from the illusory laws of the world to the one true
law of the mind. It is the change from the special
to the holy relationship, from the ego's principle of
one or the other, the shadow of the ego's thought
system of 1 + 1 = 2, to the Holy Spirit's *together, or*

not at all (T-19.IV-D.12:8), the reflection of Heaven's
$1 + 1 = 1$.

Coming back to the theme of pain and suffering,
nowhere is the difference between our two equations
more dramatically seen than in understanding
the causes of our distress—both individually and
societally. As we have seen, our decision for guilt is
the sole cause of pain, coupled with our wish to be
unfairly treated. Thus, Jesus cautions us: "Beware of
the temptation to perceive yourself unfairly treated"
(T-26.X.4:1). Following the ego's dictates, we
happily choose to be unfairly treated so as to blame
others for our perceived sins, ensuring their sin would
be punished and our sinlessness rewarded: "In this
view, you seek to find an innocence that is not Theirs
[God's and Christ's] but yours alone, and at the cost of
someone else's guilt" (T-26.X.4:2). This exemplifies
the ego's law of winners and losers: you lose so I
gain. Yet, this law is but one more illustration of the
ego's use of magic, the attempt to solve a problem
where it is not.

The distinction between $2 + 2 = 4$ and $2 + 2 = 5$
is the same distinction as between *magic* and the
miracle. Magic treats only the external, following the
laws of $2 + 2 = 4$, which are true only within the world

of illusion. However, the miracle corrects the illusion by recognizing it as such:

> A miracle is a correction. It does not create, nor really change at all. It merely looks on devastation, and reminds the mind that what it sees is false (W-pII.13.1:1-3).

Nothing need be changed in the $2 + 2 = 4$ world, or its source in the $1 + 1 = 2$ thought system of the ego. What does require change is the *belief* that there is, in truth, a $1 + 1 = 2$ reality, let alone its projection of a $2 + 2 = 4$ world.

It is essential to note that there is in fact only *one* special relationship, which is between the mind's decision maker and the ego; and *one* holy relationship, which is between the mind's decision maker and the Holy Spirit. That is all. All relationships—special or holy—that seem to exist in the ego's world of $2 + 2 = 4$ are but shadows or reflections of the mind's choice. That is all. Jesus' repeated exhortations in his course that we forgive our brothers must therefore be understood symbolically as words that meet us in the condition in which we think we exist (T-25.I.7:4). In other words, since we are unaware of our minds— the home of the ego and Holy Spirit—we are equally unaware that our bodily existence is truly an illusion:

a projection or extension of the decision for the special or holy relationship. And so Jesus speaks to us *as if* we were here; judging and forgiving, separating and joining. Yet he teaches us, too, to see our experiences here as outside pictures of an inward condition (T-21.in.1:5): projections or extensions of the mind's decision. Thus instructed, we are able at last to choose again and take our place among the teachers of God:

> A teacher of God is anyone who chooses to be one. His qualifications consist solely in this; somehow, somewhere he has made a deliberate choice in which he did not see his interests as apart from someone else's (M-1.1:1-2).

By so choosing, we join those right-minded individuals who come to reflect the oneness that is the law of the Mind:

> God's laws do not obtain directly to a world perception rules, for such a world could not have been created by the Mind to which perception has no meaning. Yet are His laws reflected everywhere....
> Here, where the laws of God do not prevail in perfect form, can he yet do *one* perfect thing and make *one* perfect choice (T-25.III.2:1-2; VI.5:1).

We have done the one perfect thing Jesus asks of us—we have chosen to forgive ourselves for mistakenly choosing the ego, thus returning our minds to the truth.

Conclusion

Considering again Dostoevsky's Underground Man, we can see how the Course provides a more right-minded alternative to his embittered alienation. Still holding to the rejection of the world's equation of $2 + 2 = 4$, the kinder and gentler teacher of God does not reject those who err in identifying with its insanity. By judging those who oppress the benighted world, Dostoevsky's protagonist ends up an oppressor as well, for he has misjudged the "enemy." His angry rebellion need not be directed at the world's thinking, insane though it may be, for it is but *his* mind's thinking that needs to be recognized and chosen against. *All* people suffer from the single oppression of choosing to be beholden to the ego's harsh and unyielding thought system of separation and judgment—its law of *one or the other*: salvation is achieved through pursuing one's own interests at the expense of someone else. And so it is the mind's identification with the thought system of $1 + 1 = 2$ that needs correction, not the projected certainty of the world of $2 + 2 = 4$.

Forgiveness and the *miracle* are the terms *A Course in Miracles* uses to describe the process of shifting from a perception of separate interests to the vision of shared interests. For this alone undoes the ego's thought system of *one or the other*: the principle of *kill or be killed* that is the shibboleth of the ego's world of $2 + 2 = 4$. Thus Jesus asks us to give up our grievances by looking at them with him. He invites us to release the temptation to "perceive ourselves unfairly treated" (T-26.X.4:1) and to make no judgments we would not apply to *all* people. He teaches us to become like him, which means perceiving no significant differences among the seemingly separated members of the Sonship. Instead, we see everyone as one, for all of us share one split mind—the ego, the Holy Spirit, and the decision maker with power to choose between them—thus re-aligning ourselves with the one Will of God and His Son: His sacred law of $1 + 1 = 1$. And so we pray:

> *Father, I thought I wandered from Your Will,*
> *defied it, broke its laws, and interposed a second*
> *will more powerful than Yours. Yet what I am in*

truth is but Your Will, extended and extending. This am I, and this will never change. As You are One, so am I one with You. And this I chose in my creation, where my will became forever one with Yours. That choice was made for all eternity. It cannot change, and be in opposition to itself. Father, my will is Yours. And I am safe, untroubled and serene, in endless joy, because it is Your Will that it be so.

Today we will accept our union with each other and our Source. We have no will apart from His, and all of us are one because His Will is shared by all of us. Through it we recognize that we are one. Through it we find our way at last to God (W-pII.329).

text

text (cont.)

text (cont.)

workbook for students

workbook for students (cont.)

workbook for students (cont.)

manual for teachers

clarification of terms

****

The Gifts of God

Foundation for A COURSE IN MIRACLES®

Kenneth Wapnick *received his Ph.D. in Clinical Psychology in 1968 from Adelphi University. He was a close friend and associate of Helen Schucman and William Thetford, the two people whose joining together was the immediate stimulus for the scribing of A COURSE IN MIRACLES. Kenneth has been involved with A COURSE IN MIRACLES since 1973, writing, teaching, and integrating its principles with his practice of psychotherapy. He is on the Executive Board of the Foundation for Inner Peace, publishers of A COURSE IN MIRACLES.*

In 1983, with his wife Gloria, he began the Foundation for A COURSE IN MIRACLES, and in 1984 this evolved into a Teaching and Healing Center in Crompond, New York, which was quickly outgrown. In 1988 they opened the Academy and Retreat Center in upstate New York. In 1995 they began the Institute for Teaching Inner Peace through A COURSE IN MIRACLES, an educational corporation chartered by the New York State Board of Regents. In 2001 the Foundation moved to Temecula, California. The Foundation publishes a quarterly newsletter, "The Lighthouse," which is available free of charge. The following is Kenneth and Gloria's vision of the Foundation.

In our early years of studying *A Course in Miracles,* as well as teaching and applying its principles in our respective professions of psychotherapy, and teaching and school administration, it seemed evident that this was not the simplest of thought systems to understand. This was so not only in the intellectual grasp of its teachings, but perhaps more importantly in the application of these teachings to our personal lives. Thus, it appeared to us from the beginning that the Course lent itself to teaching, parallel to the ongoing teachings of the Holy Spirit in the daily opportunities within our relationships, which are discussed in the early pages of the manual for teachers.

One day several years ago while Helen Schucman and I (Kenneth) were discussing these ideas, she shared a vision that she had had of a teaching center as a white temple with a gold cross atop it. Although it was clear that this image was symbolic, we understood it to be representative of what the teaching center was to be: a place where the person of Jesus and his message in *A Course in Miracles* would be manifest. We have sometimes seen an image of a lighthouse shining its light into the sea, calling to it those passers-by who sought it. For us, this light is the Course's teaching of forgiveness, which we would hope to share with those who are drawn to the Foundation's form of teaching and its vision of *A Course in Miracles*.

This vision entails the belief that Jesus gave the Course at this particular time in this particular form for several reasons. These include:

1) the necessity of healing the mind of its belief that attack is salvation; this is accomplished through forgiveness, the undoing of our belief in the reality of separation and guilt.

2) emphasizing the importance of Jesus and/or the Holy Spirit as our loving and gentle Teacher, and developing a personal relationship with this Teacher.

3) correcting the errors of Christianity, particularly where it has emphasized suffering, sacrifice, separation, and sacrament as being inherent in God's plan for salvation.

Our thinking has always been inspired by Plato (and his mentor Socrates), both the man and his teachings. Plato's Academy was a place where serious and thoughtful people came to study his philosophy in an atmosphere conducive to their learning, and then returned to their professions to implement what they were taught by the great philosopher. Thus, by integrating abstract philosophical ideals with experience, Plato's school seemed to be the perfect model for the teaching center that we directed for so many years.

We therefore see the Foundation's principal purpose as being to help students of *A Course in Miracles* deepen their understanding of its thought system, conceptually and experientially, so that they may be more effective instruments of Jesus' teaching in their own lives. Since teaching forgiveness without experiencing it is empty, one of the Foundation's specific goals is to help facilitate the process whereby people may be better able to know that their own sins are forgiven and that they are truly loved by God. Thus is the Holy Spirit able to extend His Love through them to others.

Foundation for A Course in Miracles®
Temecula, California

Please see our Web site, www.facim.org, for a complete listing of publications and available translations. You may also write, or call our office for information:

Foundation for A COURSE IN MIRACLES®
41397 Buecking Drive
Temecula, CA 92590
(951) 296-6261 • fax (951) 296-5455